THE HEALING FOODS
COOKBOOK

Also by Gary Null

Reboot Your Brain: A Natural Approach to Fighting Memory Loss, Dementia, Alzheimer's, Brain Aging, and More

No More Cancer: A Complete Guide to Preventing, Treating, and Overcoming Cancer

No More Diabetes: Preventing and Reversing Diabetes Naturally

THE HEALING FOODS
COOKBOOK

Vegan Recipes to Heal and Prevent Diabetes, Alzheimer's, Cancer, and More

GARY NULL, Ph.D.

Gary Null Publishing

Gary Null Publishing books may be purchased in bulk at special discounts for sales promotion, corporate gifts, fund-raising, or educational purposes. Special editions can also be created to specifications. For details, contact the Special Sales Department, Gary Null Publishing, 307 West 36th Street, 11th Floor, New York, NY 10018 or info@skyhorsepublishing.com.

Gary Null Publishing is an imprint of Skyhorse Publishing, Inc.

Skyhorse® and Skyhorse Publishing® are registered trademarks of Skyhorse Publishing, Inc.®, a Delaware corporation.

Visit our website at www.skyhorsepublishing.com.

10 9 8 7 6 5 4 3 2 1

Library of Congress Cataloging-in-Publication Data is available on file.
ISBN: 978-1-5107-0520-3
e-ISBN: 978-1-5107-0521-0

Cover design by Jane Sheppard

Printed in the United States of America

Introduction

The inspiration to write this cookbook stems from the more than forty years I've spent in public health as a nutritionist, dietician, professor of nutrition, and research scientist in anti-aging medicine. Throughout the decades I've devoted to studying nutrition, I have found one diet that consistently supports good health for the long term. I like to call it the Living Foods Diet.

The Living Foods Diet is a plant-based, whole foods regimen that emphasizes fresh and unprocessed organic foods. It is high in fiber and enzymes, moderate in protein and healthy fats, and abundant in healing nutrients. Even though some of the foods may be cooked, they are cooked at a temperature that is low enough to maintain the nutritional integrity of the food. The Living Foods Diet is also rich in superfoods—nutritional powerhouses like pomegranate, acai, goji, mangosteen, spirulina, and chlorella. Superfoods are packed with high amounts of phytonutrients,

chlorophylls, and antioxidants, all of which help to slow the aging process, repair DNA, boost immunity, and detoxify the body.

Most cookbooks on the market today feature recipes typical of the Standard American Diet: high in animal protein and simple carbohydrates, which can form cancer-causing heterocyclic amines or acrylamides, respectively, when cooked at high temperatures. The inclusion of sugar, wheat, eggs, dairy, meat, salt, and trans fats in conventional recipes goes far beyond what our body can possibly benefit from and metabolize. America's love affair with pro-inflammatory, sugars, fats, animal proteins, preservatives, additives, and high-temperature cooking has given rise to an abundance of food that may taste good but brings devastating health consequences.

Historically, people have thought of healthy food as boring and uninspired, offering little more than rice and beans with apple

Table of Contents

juice and a few carrots. People didn't expect to eat gourmet and exciting healthy food, and for years, they didn't. I know this because in 1972 I opened the first gourmet vegetarian restaurant in America, The Fertile Earth, at 108th Street and Broadway in Manhattan. Back then, many vegetarians feared they wouldn't get enough protein. This is because we have been indoctrinated to think that protein is the most important nutrient, despite the fact that most Americans daily consume two to three times more carbohydrates, sugars, and protein than the ideal amounts. As rates of chronic degenerative disease rise around the country, it's more important than ever to dispel the myths surrounding a plant-based diet and get people excited about choosing foods that truly can be both nutritious and gourmet.

Having counseled tens of thousands of individuals, lectured before millions of people, and conducted more than thirty health support groups for thousands of participants, I have witnessed the extraordinary restorative power of the Living Foods Diet. This same diet has formed the basis of the lifestyle protocol I've given to all the people who have come to me seeking health advice. Regardless of whether they were dealing with arthritis, obesity, cancer, or any other illness, the Living Foods Diet was the regimen they followed. Each of the recipes in this cookbook were served at a series of my health retreats over the last few years. We've witnessed people make remarkable improvements in their health by eating these foods, including individuals going from diabetic to nondiabetic and reversing the symptoms of autoimmune disease.

To make this cookbook even more beneficial, I've included specific nutrient supplementation protocols for some of the most important health issues facing Americans today: diabetes, cognitive diseases, obesity, pain, cancer, allergies, and aging. Recent reports indicate that about half of all adults in America are either prediabetic or diabetic. Meanwhile, more than 500,000 Americans die from cancer each year, and tens of millions more contend with debilitating allergies. We are also in the midst of an epidemic of neurodegenerative diseases such as dementia, Parkinson's disease, ALS, multiple sclerosis, and Alzheimer's disease. Obesity rates have reached frighteningly high levels, with four out of ten American adults and two out of ten American children falling into the category of obese. The baby boomer generation is struggling with a host of age-related conditions such as pain, fatigue, insomnia, menopause and memory loss. The incidence of depression and anxiety disorders has similarly reached record highs, affecting tens of millions of young, middle-aged, and elderly people. All of these conditions are given special attention in our targeted protocol sections, which include testimonials from people who have experienced the life-changing benefits of eating a Living Foods Diet and following these protocols.

My last cookbook, the *Anti-Arthritis, Anti-Inflammation Cookbook*, received a tremendous response after it was released in 2013. This proved to me that people are hungry for creative plant-based cuisine that supports their health and healing. With this book, you're getting even more delicious recipes, more transformative lifestyle guidance, and more empowerment to live well. The Living Foods Diet is about bringing vibrant, invigorating energy into your life, and that's what you're going to find in each and every bite.

Glossary of Vegan Ingredients

Amaranth: A high-protein grain native to Central and South America that has more fiber than wheat and rice. The grain was grown for nearly eight thousand years until it virtually disappeared for reasons unknown, in the early 1500s. Renewed interest in this tasty grain has revived its cultivation.

Barley: A grain often lower in fiber than other grains, but one of the easiest to digest. Its tough outer hull makes barley almost impossible to cook and is removed in a process called "pearling."

Basmati rice: A variety of rice grown in India that has a distinctive nutty flavor and comes in both brown and white varieties.

Cardamom: An East Indian plant whose seeds are used to produce a ground powder for a distinct Asian flavor.

Carob powder/Carob chips: Carob is the seedpod of the Mediterranean evergreen tree. It can be ground into a powder or made into chips that taste like and can be used like cocoa and chocolate chips.

Chickpeas/Garbanzo beans: A bean grown in the Mediterranean and used in such Middle Eastern dishes as hummus.

Cilantro: Also known as coriander or Chinese parsley. Used in Asian and Latin American cooking. Cilantro is the leafy portion of the plant.

Coriander: A spice made from the ground seeds of the cilantro plant. Used in Asian dishes.

Daikon: A variety of large, white Oriental radish.

Gomasio: A traditional Japanese seasoning composed of lightly toasted and ground sesame seeds and sea salt.

Kasha: Also known as buckwheat, kasha is available in both whole and unhulled forms and is found either roasted or cut.

Millet: A variety of grain high in protein and well tolerated by people allergic to other grains.

Quinoa: A high-protein grain with a unique texture.

Rice noodles: Noodles made from rice flour.

Saffron threads: The dried stigmas of the flower *Crocus sativus* used to color foods and as a cooking spice.

Sea salt: From the sea or ocean, sea salt contains trace vitamins and minerals.

Sesame oil, hot: Has a pleasant nutty flavor. Makes a good salad oil. Hot red pepper is added to create the hot spicy flavor.

Sesame oil, toasted: Made from toasted sesame seeds ground into oil.

Sesame seeds: The seeds from the sesame plant. An excellent source of protein, unsaturated fatty acids, calcium, magnesium, niacin, and vitamins A and E.

Shiitake mushrooms: One of the variety of mushrooms used in soups, salads, and main dishes. These can be purchased in most grocery stores.

Silken tofu: A creamy variety of soybean curd.

Sunflower seeds: A rich source of protein, unsaturated fatty acids, phosphorus, calcium, iron, fluorine, iodine, potassium, magnesium, zinc, some of the B vitamins, and vitamins D and E.

Tahini: Sesame seeds that have been ground into a paste.

Tamari: Naturally fermented soy sauce, 9 to 18 percent complete protein and easily digestible. It contains B vitamins, riboflavin, and niacin and is the best nonmeat source of vitamin B_{12}. Also available in wheat-free form.

Tempeh: A fermented soybean product.

Salads, Small Plates, and Sides

African Millet Salad 16

Indian Arugula Salad 17

Healthy Wild Atlantic Nori 19

Endive with Basil and Sprouts 21

Cucumber-Arame Salad 22

Mango Salad 23

Green Barley Split Salad 25

Cheese-Apple Salad 26

Arame Fennel Salad 27

Fennel and Asparagus Salad 28

Mixed Sprout Salad 29

Wakame Salad 30

Spicy Arugula-Endive Salad 31

Watercress, Orange, and Endive Salad 32

Asparagus Salad 33

Cucumber, Red Onion, and Dill Salad 34

Garden Buckwheat Salad 35

Pear Beet Salad 36

Wild Rice Salad 37

Chickpea and Lima Bean Salad 38

Mediterranean Cannellini Salad 39

Indian Potato Salad 40

Curry Dressing 41

African Millet Salad

SERVES: 2

INGREDIENTS:

1 cup adzuki beans, cooked and chilled

2 teaspoons mint

1 cup millet, cooked and chilled

1 cup red pepper, chopped

½ cup sweet onion, small diced

1 teaspoon celery salt

1 teaspoon tarragon

2 tablespoons toasted sesame oil

DIRECTIONS:

1. In a large bowl, combine beans, mint, millet, red pepper, onion, celery salt, and tarragon. Mix well.

2. Drizzle sesame oil over salad.

3. Serve chilled.

Indian Arugula Salad

SERVES: 2-4

INGREDIENTS:

3 cups cucumbers, peeled and chopped

2 cups plain nondairy yogurt

1½ cups tomatoes, chopped

1 cup fresh arugula, torn

1 tablespoon lemon juice

1 tablespoon flaxseed oil

1 teaspoon cardamom, ground

1 teaspoon apple cider vinegar

½ teaspoon sea salt

¼ cup toasted sesame seeds

2 teaspoons turmeric

¼ teaspoon cayenne pepper

DIRECTIONS:

1. In a large bowl, combine cucumbers, nondairy yogurt, tomatoes, and arugula. Mix well.

2. In a small bowl, whisk together the remaining ingredients to create the dressing.

3. Toss the salad with the dressing.

4. Serve at room temperature.

Healthy Wild Atlantic Nori

SERVES: 2

INGREDIENTS:

2 tablespoons toasted sesame oil

1 cup carrots, peeled and thinly sliced

½ cup daikon, peeled and diced

1 tablespoon tamari soy sauce

1 teaspoon lemon juice

1-ounce package laver (wild Atlantic nori) soaked in water for 1 to 2 minutes then drained and chopped fine

½ teaspoon fresh ginger, peeled and minced

1 scallion, chopped

DIRECTIONS:

1. Add sesame oil to a skillet and sauté carrots over moderate heat for 5 to 7 minutes.

2. Add daikon, tamari, lemon juice, laver, ginger, and scallions. Cook an additional 1 to 2 minutes.

3. Serve at room temperature or chilled.

Chinese medicine has long recognized the value of seaweed for treating cancers, as it impacts hardened tumors. More recently, research has shed light on the powerful mix of micronutrients, including Vitamin C and Vitamin E, as well as minerals, iodine, fiber, and polysaccharides in seaweed, which make it a powerful nutritional tool in combating cancer. Considered to be one of the healthiest populations on earth, the Japanese consume more seaweed than any other nation. In particular, Okinawans traditionally have a diet of low-fat, low-salt foods, such as fish, tofu, and seaweed. Such eating not only keeps them fit but grants them longevity. Five times as many Okinawans live to be 100 as compared to the Japanese on the mainland, and the Japanese are already the longest-living people in the world.

Endive with Basil and Sprouts

SERVES: 2

INGREDIENTS:

1 cup curly or Belgian endive, chopped

1 cup Mesclun lettuce, torn

½ cup fresh basil, firmly packed

½ cup clover sprouts

1 cup fresh tomatoes, chopped

1 cup blueberries, as garnish

½ cup pears, diced, as garnish

½ cup toasted pumpkin seeds, as garnish

DIRECTIONS:

1. In a large salad bowl, combine the endive, lettuce, basil, sprouts, and tomatoes.

2. Garnish with blueberries, pears, and pumpkin seeds.

3. Serve with a favorite salad dressing.

ELAINE

I feel energetic, attractive, and strong. The changes I was able to make during this protocol were more marked than any changes I have been able to make in several years. I followed the protocol closely, and I no longer get headaches, whereas before I usually got at least one severe headache a month. I lost twelve pounds and several inches from my hips and waist. My blood pressure dropped to 102/60. My self-confidence and energy level rose to a new high. I received many comments on my shiny hair, and people commented on how nice my skin was. I feel more confident, positive, and clearheaded, and able to focus on other life goals. I feel like a different person: stronger, happier, and enthusiastic.

Cucumber–Arame Salad

SERVES: 4

INGREDIENTS:

4 cups soaked arame

1 cup carrot, steamed and small diced

1 cup cucumber, sliced

½ cup yellow pepper, sliced

¼ sesame seeds

¼ cup apple cider vinegar

3 tablespoons extra virgin olive oil

3 tablespoons mustard

2 tablespoons date or maple sugar

1 tablespoon lemon juice

⅛ teaspoon cayenne pepper

DIRECTIONS:

1. In a large bowl, combine arame, carrot, cucumber, pepper, and sesame seeds.

2. In a small bowl, whisk together the remaining ingredients.

3. Drizzle over salad and toss well.

4. Serve immediately.

Mango Salad

SERVES: 2

INGREDIENTS:

10 ounces mango, peeled and cubed

4 ounces clover sprouts

1 cup walnuts

½ cup flaked unsweetened coconut

⅓ cup hazelnut oil

The juice of two lemons

1 teaspoon sea salt

DIRECTIONS:

Combine all ingredients in a large mixing bowl and toss well.

Green Barley Split Salad

SERVES: 3

INGREDIENTS:

6 ounces split peas, cooked

6 ounces spinach, chopped coarsely

6 ounces barley, cooked

6 ounces asparagus, cut into 1-inch
  pieces

3 tablespoons extra virgin olive oil

1 teaspoon minced garlic

½ teaspoon sea salt

DIRECTIONS:

1. Preheat oven to 375°F.

2. Lightly grease a 4 x 8 baking pan with sunflower oil.

3. Combine all ingredients together. Toss and mix well.

4. Transfer to baking pan and bake for 15 minutes or until thoroughly heated.

HOZANA
Before
I was slightly overweight and had acute heartburn, acid reflux, and stress and anger toward my teenage son. I am a massage therapist, and I wanted to change my life and learn proper nutrition, so I joined Gary's support group.

Now
I've lost 8 lbs and now have the body I've always wanted. I take organic, vegetarian juices. I no longer have acid reflux. My mind is clearer. I have a successful relationship with my son, and I handle cow-orkers without anger. I exercise by power-walking and my body is alive and energetic. I've uncluttered my mind and my home. Now, I am more open and accepting, less critical, more optimistic and helpful to people.

Cheese-Apple Salad

SERVES: 6-8

INGREDIENTS:

2 cups apples, cored and diced

8 ounces nondairy Swiss cheese, cut into strips

1 cup shredded nondairy cheddar cheese (4 ounces)

1 cup celery, blanched and diced

½ cup vegan mayonnaise

2 tablespoons lemon juice

$\frac{1}{8}$ teaspoon pepper

Lettuce

DIRECTIONS:

1. In a large bowl combine the diced apples, cheeses, celery, vegan mayonnaise, lemon juice, and pepper.

2. Toss to combine and chill.

3. Serve on a bed of lettuce.

Arame Fennel Salad

SERVES: 2

INGREDIENTS:

1 cup arame

½ cup fennel, chopped

½ cup daikon radish, shredded

¼ cup toasted sesame oil

6 tablespoons rice vinegar or apple cider vinegar

2 tablespoons lemon juice

1 teaspoon sea salt

¼ teaspoon freshly black pepper

2 tablespoons sesame seeds

DIRECTIONS:

1. In a large sauce pan, cover arame with water and boil for 15 minutes.

2. Rinse under cool water.

3. Drain and measure 1 cup.

4. In a large bowl, combine arame, fennel, and daikon radish. Mix to combine.

5. In a small bowl, whisk together sesame oil, vinegar, lemon juice, salt, and pepper.

6. Pour over arame mixture, add sesame seeds, and toss well.

7. Chill for 1 hour before serving.

Fennel and Asparagus Salad

SERVES: 2

INGREDIENTS:

¼ cup extra virgin olive oil

2 tablespoons fresh lemon juice

⅓ cup fresh orange juice

¼ teaspoon salt

¼ teaspoon freshly ground black pepper

⅓ pound endive, separated into leaves

½ pound asparagus, peeled into strips and blanched

1 pound fennel, white part thinly sliced

2 tablespoons fennel fronds, stemmed and chopped

2 tablespoons pine nuts, toasted

DIRECTIONS:

1. Blend olive oil, lemon juice, orange juice, salt, and pepper until well incorporated. Set aside.

2. Combine endive, asparagus, fennel, fennel fronds, and pine nuts in a mixing bowl.

3. Drizzle dressing over salad and toss.

4. Serve immediately.

Mixed Sprout Salad

SERVES: 2

INGREDIENTS:

2½ cups mixed crunchy sprouts
1½ cups sunflower sprouts
1 cup yellow pepper, sliced
½ cup heart of palm, quartered
½ cup artichoke hearts, quartered
2 beets, roasted and quartered
½ sweet onion, sliced
Salad dressing to taste

DIRECTIONS:

1. In a large mixing bowl, add all ingredients except for salad dressing.

2. Drizzle salad dressing and toss.

3. Serve at room temperature.

Wakame Salad

SERVES: 2

INGREDIENTS:

One package alaria (wild atlantic wakame), or 2 ounces

¾ pounds carrots, peeled and julienned

1 small red onion, chopped fine

3 tablespoons toasted sesame oil

2 teaspoons finely chopped peeled ginger

1 tablespoon black sesame seeds

The juice of two lemons

2 teaspoons tamari soy sauce

1 teaspoon sea salt

DIRECTIONS:

1. In a medium sized saucepan, bring 1½ quarts water to a boil. Add the wakame and simmer for 20 minutes. Drain and chop fine.

2. In a medium sized saucepan, simmer the carrots in a couple of cups of water for 8 minutes, then drain.

3. Sauté the onion in the oil with the ginger for 10–15 minutes until the onions are translucent. Add the wakame, carrots, sesame seeds, lemon juice, tamari, and salt. Stir until well combined.

4. Serve over cooked white quinoa.

Spicy Arugula-Endive Salad

SERVES: 2

INGREDIENTS:

1 cup beets, shredded

2 cups endive, chopped

1 cup baby arugula

1 cup yellow pepper, sliced

1 cup spicy sprouts

¾ cup fresh Italian parsley, chopped

²/₃ cup red cabbage, shredded

¼ teaspoon cayenne pepper

1 cup fresh tomatoes, diced, as garnish

DIRECTIONS:

1. In a large salad bowl, combine beets, endive, arugula, pepper, sprouts, parsley, cabbage, and cayenne. Toss thoroughly.

2. Garnish with diced tomatoes.

3. Serve with a strong lemon or vinaigrette dressing.

PAT

I was hospitalized three times for congestive heart disease. I was on oxygen 24 hours a day for emphysema. I weighed 225 pounds. I had arthritis, diabetes, sciatica, glaucoma, and used steroids.

I came to support group meetings in a wheel-chair with oxygen hook ups. Today I call myself "A Walking Miracle." I follow the protocol, walk daily, no longer use steroids, and even traveled to New York City. It took awhile to clean my system out, but vegan organic living was the answer. My neighbors are happy to see me as I leave for my daily stroll. Detoxification works.

Watercress, Orange, and Endive Salad

SERVES: 2

INGREDIENTS:

1 cup red, yellow, and orange bell
  peppers, sliced

1 cup endive, chopped

2 seedless oranges, sliced

1 cup sunflower sprouts

$^2/_3$ cup carrots, shredded

1 cup watercress

¾ cup fresh Italian parsley, chopped

1 cup fresh yellow tomatoes, chopped,
  as garnish

DIRECTIONS:

1. In a large salad bowl, combine peppers, endive, oranges, sprouts, carrots, watercress, and parsley.

2. Garnish with chopped tomatoes, if desired.

3. Serve with a vinaigrette or light lemon dressing.

Asparagus Salad

SERVES: 6-8

INGREDIENTS:

1 pound green asparagus

1 pound white asparagus

¼ cup extra virgin olive oil

¼ cup fresh lemon juice

¼ teaspoon sea salt

¼ teaspoon black pepper

¼ cup pickled ginger

1 teaspoon wasabi powder

DIRECTIONS:

1. Trim bottoms of asparagus. Place in a medium pan and blanch 3 minutes.

2. In a small bowl, whisk together olive oil, lemon juice, salt, pepper, pickled ginger, and wasabi powder.

3. Arrange asparagus on a platter and drizzle with dressing.

Cucumber, Red Onion, and Dill Salad

SERVES: 4

INGREDIENTS:

1 pound cucumbers, thinly sliced

1 medium red onion, thinly sliced

3 tablespoons fresh dill, chopped

¼ cup apple cider vinegar

2 tablespoons extra virgin olive oil

½ teaspoon garlic salt

⅛ teaspoon freshly ground black pepper

DIRECTIONS:

1. Toss all ingredients together in a mixing bowl.

2. Serve immediately.

Garden Buckwheat Salad

SERVES: 2

INGREDIENTS:

3 cups buckwheat noodles, cooked

1 cup broccoli florets, steamed 5 to 6 minutes

1 cup carrots sliced

¼ cup gomasio

2 tablespoons scallions, sliced

2 tablespoons golden raisins

2 tablespoons sunflower seeds

¼ cup toasted sesame oil

4 tablespoons tamari

DIRECTIONS:

1. In a medium size bowl, combine noodles, broccoli, carrots, gomasio, scallions, raisins, and sunflower seeds.

2. Add sesame oil and tamari. Mix well.

3. Serve chilled.

Pear Beet Salad

SERVES: 2

INGREDIENTS:

1 cup pears, sliced

1½ cups leeks, sliced and steamed 10 minutes

2 tablespoons fresh arugula, chopped

2 tablespoons fresh fennel, chopped

¼ cup olive oil

2 tablespoons prepared mustard

1 tablespoon fresh lemon juice

½ teaspoon cayenne pepper

½ cup beets, sliced and steamed for 15 minutes

DIRECTIONS:

1. In a large salad bowl, combine the pears, leeks, arugula, and fennel.

2. In a separate bowl, whisk together olive oil, mustard, lemon juice, and cayenne pepper.

3. Toss beets in ¼ of the dressing and the remaining salad with the rest of dressing.

4. Arrange beets on plate and top with rest of salad.

5. Chill for 1 hour before serving.

Wild Rice Salad

SERVES: 4

INGREDIENTS:

2 cups broccoli florets, blanched

3 cups wild rice, cooked

1 cup carrots, sliced and blanched

1 cup zucchini, diced

⅓ cup red onion, diced

¼ cup safflower oil

2 tablespoons fresh dill, chopped

¼ cup plus 1 tablespoon fresh lemon juice

1 teaspoon freshly ground black pepper

1 teaspoon sea salt

DIRECTIONS:

1. Combine all ingredients in a mixing bowl and toss until well mixed.

2. Serve at room temperature.

Chickpea and Lima Bean Salad

SERVES: 2

INGREDIENTS:

1 ounce dulse, dry

3 ounces green peas, cooked (chilled)

3 ounces chickpeas, cooked (chilled)

3 ounces lima beans, cooked (chilled)

2 tablespoons safflower oil

1 tablespoon dill, chopped

1 teaspoon tarragon, chopped

½ teaspoon sea salt

3 tablespoons lemon juice

DIRECTIONS:

1. Soak dulse in hot water for 5 minutes, then rinse under cool water and squeeze excess water out.

2. Mix all ingredients together.

3. Serve chilled.

Mediterranean Cannellini Salad

SERVES: 4

INGREDIENTS:

2 cups cannellini beans, cooked

2 cloves garlic, peeled and minced

1 tablespoon lemon juice

1 tablespoon thyme

1 tablespoon rosemary, chopped

2 scallions, chopped

6 ounces crunchy sprouts

⅛ cup balsamic vinegar or lemon juice

⅓ cup extra virgin olive oil to taste

½ tablespoon Dijon mustard

¼ teaspoon sea salt

¼ teaspoon freshly ground black pepper

2 cups field greens

DIRECTIONS:

1. In a large bowl, combine beans, garlic, lemon juice, thyme, rosemary, scallions, and crunchy sprouts.

2. In a separate bowl, add the remaining ingredients, except for the field greens, and whisk to combine.

3. Drizzle over salad and toss.

4. Serve on a bed of field greens.

Indian Potato Salad

SERVES: 4

INGREDIENTS:

2½ pounds assorted potatoes (a variety for color, taste, and texture)

⅓ cup crunchy sprouts

⅓ cup fresh parsley, chopped

½ cup olive oil

⅙ cup balsamic vinegar

⅛ cup tamari or wheat-free soy sauce

2 teaspoons cayenne pepper

1 teaspoon cumin

½ teaspoon sea salt

½ teaspoon freshly ground black pepper

DIRECTIONS:

1. Bake potatoes at 400°F for 40 minutes, or until soft (insert fork to see how easily it goes through potatoes). Allow potatoes to cool completely.

2. Cut potatoes into large chunks, approximately 6 to 8 chunks per potato. Place potatoes in a large bowl. Add sprouts and parsley.

3. In a separate bowl, whisk together olive oil, vinegar, tamari, cayenne pepper, cumin, salt, and pepper.

4. Drizzle dressing over potato salad and toss to combine.

5. Serve chilled.

Curry Dressing

MAKES: 1½ cups

INGREDIENTS:

12 ounces nondairy sour cream

3 tablespoons nondairy mayonnaise

4 teaspoons curry powder

1 teaspoon powdered ginger

½ teaspoon salt

DIRECTIONS:

1. Put all the ingredients in a blender.

2. Process until smooth.

JESSIE

I am an eighty-six-year-old woman. My blood pressure was high. My energy was very low. I felt old. My hands were full of age spots. I felt quite discouraged. I joined a Gary Null support group. Once I felt the impact of group interaction I began to feel optimistic about my future.

I keep to Gary's protocol. My emotional and physical changes are wonderful. I feel younger and free. I eat organically; I juice and exercise multiple times a week. My blood pressure has lowered and energy has increased. The age spots are lighter. My physical improvements created emotional improvements. I am grateful for this second chance.

Salad Dressing with Garlic

MAKES: 1 cup

INGREDIENTS:

¼ cup apple cider vinegar

2 teaspoons dry mustard

1 teaspoon garlic, minced

1 teaspoon paprika

¼ teaspoon sea salt

¼ teaspoon freshly ground black pepper

1 cup safflower oil

DIRECTIONS:

1. Put vinegar, mustard, garlic, paprika, salt, and pepper to taste, in a mixing bowl.

2. Add oil, beating with wire whisk.

3. Chill and serve over a favorite salad.

Creamy French Dressing

MAKES: 3 cups

INGREDIENTS:

2 cups extra virgin olive oil

1 clove garlic

2 teaspoons onion, grated

½ teaspoon dry mustard

⅛ teaspoon pepper

1 teaspoon paprika

1 teaspoon sea salt

¼ cup tomato juice

¾ cup vinegar

1 tablespoon egg replacer

DIRECTIONS:

1. Place all ingredients in a blender and process until smooth.

2. Transfer to a tightly covered jar and store in the refrigerator.

Basic Vinaigrette

MAKES: 1¼ cups

INGREDIENTS:

¼ cup balsamic vinegar or lemon juice

1 cup extra virgin olive oil, to taste

1 tablespoon Dijon mustard

½ teaspoon sea salt

¼ teaspoon ground black pepper

DIRECTIONS:

1. Whisk ingredients together.

2. Drizzle dressing over salad before tossing.

3. Serve immediately.

> **RUTH**
> To date, I can happily report wonderful changes on Gary's protocol.
> I lost 18 lbs, and my blood pressure returned to normal. My energy
> level increased, and I am not sluggish after meals. Feeling and thinking
> in a positive mode has increased my self-esteem; I feel good about
> myself. I did not regain weight, because I am determined to continue the
> program.

California Marinade

SERVES: 2

INGREDIENTS:

3 ounces cauliflower florets, in bite size pieces

3 ounces bulgur, cooked (chilled)

3 ounces avocado, cut into ½-inch cubes

1½ ounces sunflower seeds

2 ounces shallots, chopped

1 ounce unsweetened shredded coconut

2 tablespoons extra virgin olive oil

1 teaspoon tarragon

½ teaspoon basil, chopped

1 teaspoon tamari

¼ teaspoon sea salt

2 teaspoons cider vinegar

DIRECTIONS:

1. Steam cauliflower for 8 minutes.

2. Combine with the remaining ingredients and mix well.

3. Serve chilled.

Because of their fat content, avocados can help you absorb nutrients from other foods more effectively. For example, low fat vegetables like sweet potatoes, carrots, spinach, and leafy greens abound in vitamins and minerals, but your body only extracts a small portion of these benefits when such foods are eaten by themselves. Healthy fats, like avocado, can bind themselves to the structures of other foods and dramatically increase the levels of nutrients your body pulls from them.

Sautéed Kale with Shiitake Mushrooms

SERVES: 2-3

INGREDIENTS:

¼ cup toasted sesame oil

1 pound kale, stems removed and cut into ribbons

1 tablespoon minced garlic

2 tablespoons minced ginger

1 large jalapeño, diced

⅓ pound shiitake mushrooms stems removed and sliced

1 tablespoon tamari

1 tablespoons agave

1 tablespoon sesame seeds

DIRECTIONS:

1. In a skillet over medium heat sauté kale, garlic, ginger, and jalapeño in toasted sesame oil for 5 minutes.

2. Add mushrooms, tamari, agave, and sauté for 5 minutes.

3. Top with sesame seeds and serve.

Stuffed Avocado

SERVES: 2

INGREDIENTS:

2 ripe medium avocados

½ cup chopped celery

¼ cup chopped fresh parsley

3 tablespoons lemon juice

¼ cup extra virgin olive oil

1 teaspoon maple syrup

¼ cup fresh basil

1 clove garlic, minced

Lettuce, carrot, and celery sticks for garnish

¼ teaspoon sea salt

DIRECTIONS:

1. Remove the pits from the avocados and carefully scoop out the pulp, saving the skin.

2. Vigorously whisk ingredients together with the avocado pulp in a large mixing bowl until smooth.

3. Fill the avocado skin with the mixture and chill.

4. Once chilled serve on a bed of lettuce with sliced carrot and celery sticks.

Apple Goji Walnut Millet

SERVES: 2

INGREDIENTS:

1 cup millet

4½ cups water

½ cup unsweetened almond milk

½ cup chopped walnuts

½ cup chopped dried apple rings

¼ cup maple syrup

¼ cup goji berries

DIRECTIONS:

1. Cook 1 cup millet in 4½ cups water in a medium-sized saucepan over moderate heat for 30 to 35 minutes.

2. Reduce heat to low and add almond milk, walnuts, apples, maple syrup, and goji berries. Cook for an additional 5 minutes.

Nuts and seeds are great brain food. They provide beneficial amounts of "intelligent" fat, the kind your body can process into healthy energy. Further, nuts and seeds are an excellent source of zinc, an essential mineral. The zinc found in these foods was removed from the soil and incorporated into living plant tissue, which make it absorbable and usable by the body's metabolism. The United States Recommended Daily Allowance (RDA) for adults is 15 mg per day. Nuts are on the lower end of the glycemic spectrum; thus, in addition to being a versatile ingredient, they are also a great snack for those with diabetes.

Some of the best nuts: walnuts, almonds, pine nuts, and pistachios. Some of the best seeds: sunflower, hemp, flax, sesame, and chia. (Walnuts, flaxseeds, and chia seeds are also high in omega-3 fatty acids, which are highly beneficial for those with chronic inflammatory diseases and circulation problems.)

Barley with Collard Greens and Leeks

SERVES: 2

INGREDIENTS:

1½ cups barley

3 cups water

½ cup sliced leeks, white parts only

½ cup sliced mushrooms

½ cups sliced collard greens

1 cup chopped fresh tomatoes

¼ cup + 1 tablespoon extra virgin olive oil

½ cup sliced red bell peppers

¼ chopped fresh parsley

1 teaspoon garlic salt

½ teaspoon celery salt

½ teaspoons freshly ground black pepper

½ teaspoon dried oregano

DIRECTIONS:

1. To cook barley, add 1½ cup barley to 3 cups of water. Cook covered for 20 minutes over moderate heat, until water is absorbed or until barley is done.

2. In a large saucepan, sauté the leeks, mushrooms, collard greens, and tomato in the oil over medium heat for 5 minutes.

3. Add the remaining ingredients, mix well, and sauté an additional 3 to 5 minutes.

4. Serve.

Coconut Nut Rice

SERVES: 2

INGREDIENTS:

¾ cup brown rice

1½ cups water

½ cup unsweetened coconut, shredded

¼ cup raw cashews, chopped

1½ ounces dried apricots, diced

¼ cup raw sunflower seeds

¼ cup golden hunza raisins

1 cup coconut milk

¼ teaspoon cinnamon

1 teaspoon vanilla extract

RICE PREPARATION:

1. Cook rice with 1½ cups water on high for 10 minutes, then lower heat to medium and continue cooking for 10 to 20 minutes until rice is done.

2. Combine brown rice with coconut, cashews, apricots, sunflower seeds, and raisins in a bowl.

3. Puree half the mixture in a food processor with coconut milk, vanilla extract, and cinnamon.

4. Add the rest of the rice.

It is especially important that the nuts and seeds you eat are organic because their oils can retain chemicals for longer periods of time than other produce.

Coleslaw with Fresh Fennel

SERVES: 2

INGREDIENTS:

3 tablespoons lemon juice

2 tablespoons lime juice

4 cups green cabbage, shredded

2¼ cups fennel bulbs sliced very thinly

⅓ cup vegan mayonnaise

1 tablespoon picked relish

1 tablespoon fresh dill, chopped

1 teaspoon sea salt

¼ teaspoon black pepper

½ teaspoon apple cider vinegar

⅛ teaspoon cayenne pepper

DIRECTIONS:

1. In a medium size mixing bowl, toss all ingredients.

2. Serve chilled as a salad or sandwich filling.

Levels of acetylcholine are known to decline with age, and studies have shown that supplementation with choline—which can be found in cabbage—can improve memory and learning.

Mrs. Kartalyan's Rice Pilaf

SERVES: 2

INGREDIENTS:

3 cups water

¾ teaspoon saffron threads

1 cup uncooked brown rice, short grain

3 tablespoons coconut oil

1 teaspoon fennel seeds

1 cup tiny rice pasta, in the shape of your choice, cooked

½ cup sliced almonds

DIRECTIONS:

1. Bring 3 cups of water to a boil.

2. Add the saffron and reduce heat to simmer.

3. In a large saucepan, sauté the rice in the oil over medium heat until it turns light brown.

4. Add the saffron water and fennel seeds to the rice and cook on low heat for 25 minutes.

5. Stir in pasta and remove from heat.

6. Add almonds and mix.

7. Serve.

Brown rice is an excellent complex carbohydrate which provides your body with a source of glucose in a healthy, gradual manner. Unlike simple carbohydrates (such as those in candy and breads), complex carbohydrates (such as those in whole grain bread and brown rice) do not contribute as radically to high blood sugar levels. Complex carbo-hydrates stabilize and improve health.

If you're watching your glucose levels, avoid white bread, short grain white rice, russet potatoes, and pumpkin. Instead, choose brown, wild, and basmati rice, couscous, barley, beans, or sweet potatoes. Several recipes throughout this cookbook utilize brown rice or suggest it as an accompa-niment to a dish, providing a healthy carbohydrate source for the meal.

Brussels Sprouts with Tempeh Bacon and Toasted Hazelnuts

SERVES: 4-6

INGREDIENTS:

2 green apples, peeled and diced

2 tablespoons fresh lemon juice

½ pound tempeh bacon (12 slices)

⅓ cup extra virgin olive oil

1 cup hazelnuts

2 pounds Brussels sprouts, trimmed and halved

¾ cup red onion, diced

1 tablespoon balsamic vinegar

½ teaspoon sea salt

¼ teaspoon black pepper

1 cup water

1 tablespoon pure maple syrup

DIRECTIONS:

1. Preheat oven to 350°F. Roast hazelnuts until golden. Remove skins by rubbing them together. Set aside.

2. In a bowl, combine apples with lemon juice.

3. In a large deep skillet, sauté tempeh bacon in ¼ cup of extra virgin olive oil over medium heat, 5 minutes each side until browned. Remove from pan, chop finely, and set aside.

4. Add Brussels sprouts, onions, balsamic vinegar, salt, and pepper to pan and cook for 5 minutes over moderate heat.

5. Add water and apples to pan. Cover and steam ingredients for 5 minutes.

6. Add tempeh bacon and continue to sauté for 10–15 minutes on low. Then add hazelnuts and maple syrup and serve.

Black Eyed Peas with Tempeh Bacon & Lemon Thyme Collard Greens

SERVES: 6-8

INGREDIENTS:

8 cups black eyed peas

¼ cup extra virgin olive oil, plus
    3 tablespoons

12 strips of tempeh bacon

3½ pounds fresh collard greens

11 cups Basic Vegetable Stock (see
    recipe on page 113)

1 cup finely diced yellow onion

½ teaspoon freshly ground black pepper

1 teaspoon sea salt

1 teaspoon lemon thyme

DIRECTIONS:

1. Rinse black eyed peas under cool water, drain, and place in a large saucepan. Cover the peas and boil for 2 to 3 minutes. Remove the saucepan from heat source and cover. Allow the peas to stand for 60 minutes and rinse. Return to saucepan and set aside.

2. In a large skillet over medium heat, add ¼ cup of the olive oil. Add the tempeh bacon and flip while cooking 5 minutes each side. When golden brown, drain on a paper towel and dice very fine. Set aside.

3. Rinse collard greens thoroughly and remove the tough center stem from each leaf. Roll each leaf up and slice into 1-inch ribbons. In a large saucepan, add enough water to fill halfway and bring to a boil. Add the collard greens (they wilt quickly) and cook until tender, about 7 to 10 minutes. Remove the collard greens and place in an ice water bath and rinse. Return the collards to the saucepan and set aside.

4. Add 9 cups of the vegetable stock to the black eyed peas and cook for 10 minutes.

5. Add the chopped tempeh bacon and onions. Cook 25 to 30 minutes over medium high heat, covered. Cook until all water is absorbed and peas are tender. Set aside.

6. Add 2 cups of the vegetable stock to the collard greens and cook over medium heat for 7 to 10 minutes. Add the seasonings and stir to combine.

7. Serve the collard greens over the peas.

Kale and Red Potatoes

SERVES: 2

INGREDIENTS:

1 tablespoon extra-virgin olive oil

1 leek, chopped

½ onion, peeled and chopped

1 clove elephant garlic or 3 regular cloves, chopped

2 cups kale, chopped

1 cup arugula, chopped

1 cup fresh watercress

¼ teaspoon powdered sage

2 russet potatoes, peeled and cubed

1 sweet potato, peeled and cubed

¼ cup potato water (see below)

Paprika as garnish

DIRECTIONS:

1. In a saucepan, heat the oil over medium heat.

2. Sauté the leek, onion, and garlic until soft, approximately 10 minutes.

3. Add kale, arugula, and watercress. Cook until tender, stirring frequently, about 5 minutes.

4. In salted water, boil potatoes until cooked through, 30 minutes.

5. Drain, reserving ¼ cup cooking water.

6. Place the potatoes in a medium size bowl, and add the sautéed greens, sage, and potato water and mash until moderately thick.

7. Garnish with a sprinkle of paprika.

8. Serve immediately.

Shiitake Basil Mashed Potatoes

SERVES: 2

INGREDIENTS:

1 cup fresh basil, packed

½ cup extra virgin olive oil, plus
   3 tablespoons

2 teaspoons fresh rosemary, chopped

Pinch of cayenne pepper

2 lbs Yukon Potatoes, quartered

¼ cup onion, diced in ½ inch pieces

1 teaspoon garlic, minced

½ pound shiitake mushrooms, stemmed
   and diced

1¼ teaspoon sea salt

¼ tsp white pepper

DIRECTIONS:

1. Process basil, ½ cup olive oil, rosemary, and cayenne pepper in a blender and set aside.

2. Cover potatoes with water in a medium saucepan and bring to a boil for 20 minutes or until they are easily pierced by a fork.

3. Strain water from potatoes, place potatoes in a mixing bowl, and add the herb mixture.

4. Using a handheld mixer or masher, whip or mash the potato mixture.

5. In a skillet, add 3 tablespoons olive oil and sauté onion, garlic, shiitake mushrooms, sea salt, and pepper on low heat until lightly browned. Mash with potatoes.

SERVING SUGGESTIONS:

Blend shiitake mushroom gravy for a more traditional, pureed gravy.

Spicy Potato Bhaji

SERVES: 2-4

INGREDIENTS:

²/₃ cup extra virgin olive oil

1 large red onion, finely chopped

3¼ pounds Yukon Gold potatoes, sliced into matchsticks and reserved in water until ready to use

3 cloves garlic, peeled and chopped

1 tablespoon ginger, peeled and grated

1½ teaspoons turmeric

1½ teaspoons curry powder

1½ teaspoons cumin

1 teaspoon cayenne pepper

¼ teaspoon red pepper flakes

2¼ teaspoons sea salt

¼ teaspoon black pepper

1 x 10 oz package frozen peas

2 jalapeño peppers, seeds removed and diced

1 bunch scallions, sliced (about 1¾ cups)

1 cup cilantro, chopped

DIRECTIONS:

1. Heat skillet for 3–4 minutes with oil over moderate to high heat. Add onions, potatoes, garlic, ginger, turmeric, curry powder, cumin, cayenne pepper, red pepper flakes, salt, and pepper. Sauté for 6–7 minutes. Cover and cook for an additional 2 minutes.

2. Add peas and cook for an additional 3–4 minutes, stirring constantly.

3. Add jalapeños, scallions, and cilantro and cook an additional 2–3 minutes.

Red Brazilian Rice

SERVES: 2

INGREDIENTS:

1 cup chopped red onion

1 cup chopped fresh tomato

1½ teaspoons drained, crushed capers

¼ cup sliced large green olives

1 bay leaf

2 tablespoons extra virgin olive oil

1½ cups brown basmati rice

2 tablespoons pumpkin seeds

¼ teaspoon dried thyme

½ teaspoons freshly ground black pepper

1 teaspoon sea salt

DIRECTIONS:

1. To cook rice, add 1½ cups rice and 4 cups water for 25 to 30 minutes over moderate heat, covered. Set aside.

2. In a large saucepan, sauté the onions, tomatoes, capers olives, and bay leaf in oil over medium heat until the onions are translucent, about 5 to 8 minutes.

3. Add the remaining ingredients and sauté another 3 to 4 minutes or until hot.

4. Serve with black beans.

Rio Rice

SERVES: 2

INGREDIENTS:

2½ tablespoons toasted sesame oil

1 cup cauliflower florets, steamed

2 tablespoons fresh parsley, chopped

2 tablespoons toasted sesame seeds

⅓ cup black beans, cooked

⅓ cup brown rice, cooked

½ teaspoon tamari

½ teaspoon sea salt

½ avocado, sliced, diced, garnish

DIRECTIONS:

1. Preheat the oven to 375°F.

2. Lightly grease a 4 x 8 inch baking pan with sesame oil.

3. Steam the cauliflower for about 5 minutes.

4. Combine cauliflower, parsley, sesame seeds, beans, rice, tamari, and sea salt. Mix well.

5. Transfer to baking pan and bake for 15 minutes.

6. Garnish with avocado slices, if desired.

7. Serve immediately.

SARAH

I went a couple of months ago for tests and my liver test came back very bad. I was very concerned. I told her I ate a lot of whole wheat bread that I baked myself from organic sources where no pesticides were used. She insisted that since I was hypoglycemic and had some trace mineral deficiencies that I could not handle refined grains. So, I stopped eating the bread and started eating brown rice and kasha instead. Also, I took out my juicer and started making juices and blending salads.

Six weeks later I went for a blood test, which was completely normal. All this happened just because I omitted the flour and drank lots of juice and water and blended salads. I am feeling much better now, thank God. I sleep much better too.

Japanese Hijiki

SERVES: 2

INGREDIENTS:

1 cup hijiki, soaked in water and drained

2 tablespoons toasted sesame oil

2 tablespoons finely chopped scallions

2 tablespoons diced red pepper

1 tablespoon tamari

DIRECTIONS:

1. Sauté hijiki for 2 minutes over medium-high heat in sesame oil.

2. Add scallions, red pepper, and tamari to skillet and reduce heat to medium for 5 minutes.

3. Serve at room temperature.

Note: This can be stored for up to 2 days in the refrigerator and served cold.

Spicy Raw Thai Roll-Ups

ROLLS: 6

INGREDIENTS:

1 cup toasted coconut, shredded

1 cup cashews

½ lime or lemon, diced

3 teaspoons Thai chili paste

6 leaves young collard greens, trimmed and steamed

DIRECTIONS:

1. In a food processor, mix together coconut, cashews, lime or lemon, and chili paste.

2. Drop 2 tablespoons of mixture on each leaf of greens and roll up.

3. Serve immediately.

KEVIN

Before my involvement in sports, I was troubled with a variety of physical ailments. I had hay fever throughout most of the early and late growing season and I was a cold-weather asthmatic as well. At the time I wasn't paying close attention to what I was eating. I was a junk-food junkie.

After I started training, however, my body demanded better food: unprocessed food, fruits, vegetables, and a lot more salads. I also cut back on red meat.

I received a lot of benefit from the combination of exercise and good nutrition. Recently, I have even been able to train in the cold weather because I am no longer suffering from asthma. I am sleeping a lot better too.

Vermont Maple Squash

SERVE: 1

INGREDIENTS:

10 ounces spaghetti squash

1 tablespoon maple syrup

1 ounce brewer's yeast

¼ teaspoon cinnamon

DIRECTIONS:

1. Preheat oven to 400°F.

2. Cut squash in half, remove the seeds and discard. Place in baking dish cut side down with ⅓ inch of water.

3. Bake for 40 minutes.

4. Remove from oven and let cool.

5. When cooled, spoon out squash and place in a bowl. Add remaining ingredients and mix well.

6. Serve.

Butternut Squash with Tofu

SERVES: 4

INGREDIENTS:

1 15-ounce package firm tofu, cut into ½-inch cubes

8 cloves garlic, peeled and chopped fine

2 tablespoons fresh ginger, peeled and finely diced

3 tablespoons toasted sesame oil

One pound butternut squash, cut into ½-inch cubes and steamed for 15–20 minutes

1 cup long grain brown rice cooked in 5 cups water for 15–20 minutes

1 gram alaria seaweed, soaked in water for 10 minutes then drained and chopped fine

6 scallions, sliced fine

1 tablespoon tamari soy sauce

1 tablespoon black sesame seeds

DIRECTIONS:

1. Sauté the tofu, garlic, and ginger in the sesame oil over moderate heat for 5–7 minutes.

2. Add the remaining ingredients and stir until well combined and heated through.

3. Serve in a baked kombucha squash.

Crunchy Herbed Green Beans

SERVES: 4-6

INGREDIENTS:

1 pound green beans
1½ cups boiling water
½ teaspoon sea salt
¼ cup onion, finely minced
½ cup green pepper, chopped
½ teaspoon marjoram leaves
½ teaspoon rosemary, finely chopped
½ teaspoon freshly ground black pepper

DIRECTIONS:

1. Snip off the ends of the green beans and steam the beans over salted water for 3 to 4 minutes, or until they are tender but not overcooked—they should be crunchy.

2. Mix the beans, onion, green pepper, and seasonings in a large bowl.

3. Serve hot.

Sicilian String Beans

SERVES: 4

INGREDIENTS:

½ cup extra virgin olive oil

1¼ pounds portobello mushrooms, sliced

1¾ pounds tomatoes, diced

¾ cup onions, diced

4 cloves garlic, minced

1½ pound string beans, trimmed and strings removed

2 teaspoons fresh oregano, chopped

2 tablespoons fresh parsley, chopped

2 teaspoons sea salt

1 teaspoon freshly ground black pepper

1 cup pine nuts, toasted

1 cup golden raisins

Dressing

½ cup fresh basil, chopped

¼ cup extra virgin olive oil

4 cloves garlic

DIRECTIONS:

1. Add olive oil to a skillet over medium heat and sauté mushrooms, tomatoes, onions, garlic, string beans, oregano, parsley, salt, and pepper. Cook for 20 minutes.

2. For dressing, add basil, olive oil, and garlic to a blender and process until smooth.

3. Remove beans from heat and toss with dressing.

4. Finish with pine nuts and golden raisins to serve.

Peas with Mushroom Gravy

SERVES: 2

INGREDIENTS:

Mashed peas

1 small red onion, peeled and diced, about ½ cup

1 small zucchini, diced, about ½ cup

3 tablespoons extra-virgin olive oil

½ teaspoon rubbed sage

Two 10-ounce packages frozen peas

½ teaspoon sea salt

1 tablespoon roasted pumpkin seeds

Mushroom gravy

2 stalks celery, diced

1 yellow onion, peeled and diced about ½ pound

½ pound shiitake mushrooms, stems discarded and tops sliced

3 tablespoons extra-virgin olive oil

3 tablespoons fresh rosemary leaves, chopped fine

One 13.5-ounce can coconut milk

½ teaspoon sea salt

¼ teaspoon white pepper

DIRECTIONS:

To make the mashed peas

1. Sauté the onion and zucchini in the olive oil over moderate heat for 15 minutes. Stir in the sage.

2. In a small saucepan, boil the peas in 3 cups water for 10 minutes. Drain and transfer to a food processor fitted with a metal blade. Process for one minute then transfer to a mixing bowl, stir in the cooked onion mixture with salt and pumpkin seeds until well combined, cover and set aside.

To make the gravy

In a sauté pan combine the celery, onion, mushrooms, and olive oil and cook over moderate heat for 7–8 minutes. Add the rosemary, coconut milk, salt, and pepper and continue to cook for 10 additional minutes. Remove from heat and pour over mashed peas.

Holiday Cranberry Sauce

QUARTS: 2

INGREDIENTS:

32 ounces freshly squeezed orange juice

2 pounds fresh cranberries

1½ cups maple syrup

1 teaspoon orange zest

⅓ cup fresh ginger juice

¼ teaspoon cloves, whole

DIRECTIONS:

1. Combine orange juice and 1 pound of the cranberries in a saucepan and cook over medium heat, uncovered, for 30 minutes.

2. Transfer to a food processor or blender and process for 2 minutes.

3. Return to saucepan and add remaining ingredients. Cook on low for 20 minutes.

4. Chill 1 hour before serving.

SERVING SUGGESTIONS

· Control the texture of your sauce by straining the liquid and adding it back to create a chunkier or saucier sauce.

Soups

Barley-Millet Soup

MAKES: 5 quarts

INGREDIENTS:

2 tablespoons extra virgin olive oil

4 leeks, sliced including green part

1 stalk celery, chopped

½ pound mushrooms, sliced

¾ cup barley

½ cup millet

3 quarts water

6 tablespoons brown rice miso

½ cup water

DIRECTIONS:

1. In a soup pot, heat the oil. Add the leeks, celery, and mushrooms. Sauté over medium heat for 10 minutes until the vegetables are tender.

2. Add the barley and millet and water.

3. Add the water and bring to a boil. Simmer for 1 hour, or until the barley is tender. Add more water if necessary to keep the barley from sticking to the bottom of the pot and stir occasionally to prevent scorching. Remove from heat.

4. Dissolve the miso in the ½ cup water and stir into the soup.

Carrot Potato Soup

SERVES: 2

INGREDIENTS:

5 carrots

2-inch piece ginger

1 lime peeled

½ cup olive oil

1½ large Vidalia onions, peeled and finely chopped (about 2 cups)

1½ tablespoon garlic, minced

4 red potatoes, diced and cooked

1 tablespoon plus 1 teaspoon grated ginger

1½ teaspoons sea salt

½ teaspoon black pepper, freshly ground

2 cups purified water

1 large lime, sliced into quarters, as garnish

⅓ cup nondairy yogurt, as garnish

2 tablespoons parsley, finely chopped, as garnish

DIRECTIONS:

1. Push the carrots, ginger, and lime through the juicer. Collect 1 cup of the pulp, and all of the juice, and set aside.

2. In a medium saucepan, heat oil and sauté the onions, garlic, potatoes, and ginger over medium heat for 7 to 8 minutes.

3. When the onions become translucent, stir in the juice mixture, pulp, salt, pepper, if desired, and water. Simmer 10 minutes.

4. Garnish with a lime wedge, a dollop of yogurt, and parsley, if desired.

5. Serve hot or chilled.

Curried Carrot Soup

SERVES: 2

INGREDIENTS:

2 tablespoons coconut oil

1 onion, chopped

2 cloves garlic, chopped

2 teaspoons curry powder

2 tablespoons spelt or rice flour

4 cups vegetable stock (see page 113)

3 carrots, tops removed, washed and chopped

½ cup carrot juice (juice 1 or 2 carrots)

1½ cups rice milk

1 tablespoon palm or date sugar

½ teaspoon cayenne pepper

1 teaspoon sea salt

½ teaspoon fresh ground pepper

2 tablespoon parsley or chives, chopped

DIRECTIONS:

1. In a large saucepan over medium heat add oil and sauté the onion and garlic with curry powder for 5 minutes. Stir in flour, the 3 carrots, and vegetable stock. Bring to a boil and simmer 30 minutes.

2. Juice carrots for ½ cup juice. Set aside.

3. Pour contents of saucepan into a blender or food processor. Blend well.

4. Return to saucepan and add carrot juice, rice milk, and palm or date sugar.

5. Add cayenne, salt, and pepper.

6. Garnish with parsley or chives. Serve hot.

Shiitake Soup

SERVES: 3

INGREDIENTS:

¼ cup olive oil

4 cups yellow onions, sliced

2 cups shiitake mushrooms, sliced with stems removed

¼ cup fresh parsley, chopped

4 cups water

2 vegetable bouillon cubes (Morga)

½ teaspoon freshly ground black pepper

1 tablespoon fresh basil, chiffonade

1½ teaspoons garlic powder

2 tablespoons sweet miso paste (see note)

DIRECTIONS:

1. In a large saucepan over medium-high heat add the oil and sauté the onions, shiitake mushrooms, and parsley until onions are translucent.

2. Add the water, bouillon, pepper, basil, and garlic powder. Stir well.

3. Reduce the heat to simmer, cover and cook for 20 minutes.

4. Remove from heat and whisk in miso paste, stirring until dissolved.

5. Serve immediately.

Note: Never simmer miso; always add miso to a recipe after the cooking process is done. There are several types of miso available; experiment and use the one you like best.

Black Bean Parsnip Soup

SERVES: 2

INGREDIENTS:

1½ cups black beans, canned, or ⅓ cup dried beans (see note)

½ cup parsnips, chopped into ½-inch cubes

4 cups purified water

1 cup corn (fresh or frozen)

1 cup tofu, cut into ½-inch cubes

3 tablespoons fresh chives, minced

3 tablespoons coconut oil

1 teaspoon sea salt

½ teaspoon cumin

DIRECTIONS:

1. In a large saucepan, heat canned beans and parsnips in 6 ounces of water and bring to a boil.

2. Add the remaining water with corn, tofu, chives, coconut oil, salt, and cumin. Mix well and bring to a boil.

3. Lower heat to medium then puree half of mixture until smooth. Add the pureed mixture back to the rest of the soup.

4. Cook for an additional 30 minutes over low heat.

5. Serve hot.

Note: If using dried beans, soak overnight in 32 ounces of water. In the morning, rinse well and add 40 ounces of fresh water. Bring beans and fresh water to a boil, lower heat to medium, and cover. Cook for about 1 hour, and then follow steps 2 to 6.

Black Bean Soup

SERVES: 4

INGREDIENTS:

3 tablespoons extra virgin oil

1 onion, chopped

2 stalks celery with leaves, chopped

1 teaspoon celery salt, or more to taste

3 cloves garlic, minced

1½ cups black beans, washed very well

6 cups vegetable stock (see page 113)

¼ cup lemon juice

DIRECTIONS:

1. In a large soup pot over medium heat add olive oil and sauté the onion, celery, celery salt, and garlic for 5 minutes until the onion is translucent and celery is wilted.

2. Add the black beans and vegetable stock. Bring the mixture to a boil. Cover and simmer for 2 hours, or until the beans are very tender.

3. Transfer half the mixture to a blender and puree. Return it to the pot and cook until it thickens slightly, about 10 minutes.

4. Remove from heat and stir in the lemon juice.

5. Serve.

It is beneficial to take garlic every day as a preventive measure and to enhance your well-being. You can take garlic tablets and use a lot of garlic in your cooking. Much research has been done on garlic in the last five to ten years to make garlic products more potent and concentrated while eliminating their effects on the breath.

Gary's Rice Noodle Soup

SERVES: 2

INGREDIENTS:

5 tablespoons extra virgin olive oil

½ cup sliced zucchini

½ cup sliced potatoes

1 cup celery, chopped

1 cup diced onions

¼ cup sliced shiitake mushrooms

¼ cup chopped fresh parsley

½ cup broccoli florets

1 teaspoon sea salt

¼ teaspoon freshly ground black pepper

2 bay leaves

¼ cup chopped fresh dill

6 cups water

2 cups cooked rice noodles

4 cloves garlic, chopped

1 vegetable bouillon cube

DIRECTIONS:

1. In a large saucepan heat oil over medium heat and sauté vegetables about 10 minutes.

2. Add remaining ingredients, except rice noodles, and let simmer over medium low heat for 25 to 30 minutes.

3. Remove from heat, add noodles, and serve.

Healing Miso Soup

SERVES: 4

INGREDIENTS:

6 cups vegetable stock or water

1 onion, chopped in ¼-inch pieces

1 tablespoon garlic, minced

14-ounce package firm tofu, diced in
  ½-inch cubes

1 teaspoon ginger, grated

1 cup shiitake mushrooms, sliced

½ cup mixed seaweed of choice (hijiki,
  kombu, kelp, nori)

1 cup chard or collard greens, cut into
  bite size chunks

2 tablespoons miso (see note)

1 tablespoon parsley, chopped

1 tablespoon wasabi

½ teaspoon cayenne pepper

3 scallions, each sliced

DIRECTIONS:

1. Bring stock to a boil and turn down heat.

2. Simmer onion, garlic, tofu, ginger, mushrooms, seaweed, and chard or collard greens in vegetable stock for 5 minutes. Turn off heat.

3. In a small bowl, whisk together 2 tablespoons of miso with ½ to 1 cup broth, until fully dissolved. Add parsley, wasabi, cayenne pepper, and scallions. Mix well.

4. Add miso mix back into original pot and stir well.

5. Serve immediately.

Note: Never simmer miso; always add miso to a recipe after the cooking process is done. There are several types of miso available; experiment and use the one you like best.

Pure Carrot Ginger Soup

SERVES: 6

INGREDIENTS:

⅓ cup extra virgin olive oil

5 pounds carrots, chopped

4 celery stalks, sliced

1 large onion, sliced

¼ cup ginger, grated

1 teaspoon sea salt

½ teaspoon freshly ground black pepper

DIRECTIONS:

1. Add olive oil to a large saucepan over medium-high heat and sauté carrots, celery, onion, and ginger for 10 minutes until a bit of browning has occurred.

2. Add 8 cups of water, salt, pepper and simmer for 30 minutes until carrots are tender.

3. Add soup to a food processor or blender in batches and puree until smooth.

ALEXANDRA
One morning I woke up filled with energy. When I started the program, I had a real lack of energy. I was sleeping 10 to 12 hours a night and was always tired by 4 pm. Now my sleep is down to six to eight hours each night. I still can't believe it.

I also lost 10 pounds just from the elimination of sugar, dairy, and wheat. I also maintain a regular exercise program.

Savory Corn, Fennel, and Potato Chowder

SERVES: 4

INGREDIENTS:

2 pounds fennel, white part sliced and
   fronds reserved for garnish

2 pounds yukon potatoes, sliced

3 celery stalks, sliced

1 large onion, sliced

½ teaspoon cayenne pepper

2 teaspoons sea salt

1 teaspoon freshly ground black pepper

¼ cup extra virgin olive oil

4 cups almond milk

10 ounces corn kernels

DIRECTIONS:

1. Preheat oven to 350°F.

2. Toss fennel, potatoes, celery, and onion in a large mixing bowl with cayenne pepper, salt, black pepper, and olive oil.

3. Arrange vegetables in a single layer on a baking sheet and bake for 35 minutes.

4. Add almond milk then corn to a blender and puree.

5. Add baked vegetables to corn puree in parts and blend until smooth.

Tofu Millet Soup

SERVES: 4

INGREDIENTS:

2 tablespoons coconut oil

1 onion, chopped

4 cloves garlic, pressed

½ cup millet

5 cups low sodium vegetable stock

2 teaspoons onion powder

2 teaspoons garlic powder

1 teaspoon chopped fresh parsley

4 tablespoons basil

1 teaspoon dill

4 teaspoon tarragon

1 teaspoon oregano

¼ to ½ pound fresh green peas, shelled

⅓ pound tofu, cut into small pieces

DIRECTIONS:

1. Heat the oil in a large heavy saucepan. Add the onion, garlic, and millet. Sauté until the onion is translucent and the garlic is golden but not browned, about 5 minutes.

2. Add the vegetable stock and spices. Bring to a boil, and then reduce to simmer. Cook for about 15 minutes or until the millet is just cooked.

3. Add the peas and tofu and simmer about 10 minutes, until the peas are cooked. Be careful not to overcook because the peas are at peak flavor when they are just tender.

Cashew Bean Soup

SERVES: 2

INGREDIENTS:

3 ounces kidney beans

6 ounces brown rice

1½ ounces cashews, chopped

3 tablespoons sunflower oil

½ teaspoon minced garlic

¼ teaspoon chili powder

2 teaspoons salt

DIRECTIONS:

1. Soak beans overnight in water. In the morning, rinse the beans, place them in a medium saucepan, and add 32 ounces of fresh water.

2. Bring to a boil and lower to medium-low heat. Cook covered.

3. After 1½ hours of cooking the beans, add the remaining ingredients.

4. Continue to cook for an additional 30 minutes.

5. Puree half of the soup in a blender and add back to the rest of the soup.

6. Cook for an additional 10 minutes.

7. Serve hot.

Cream of Cauliflower-Broccoli Soup

SERVES: 2

INGREDIENTS:

2 cups rice milk or coconut milk

1 cup potatoes, cubed and steamed
15 minutes, until tender

1 cup broccoli florets, steamed
6 minutes

½ cup cauliflower florets, steamed
6 minutes

1 cup water

1 teaspoon sea salt

¼ teaspoon freshly ground black pepper

½ teaspoon fresh rosemary, chopped

¼ cup onions, diced

1½ teaspoons tamari

DIRECTIONS:

1. In a blender, combine rice or coconut milk, potatoes, broccoli, cauliflower, water, salt, pepper, rosemary, onions, and tamari. Blend until smooth.

2. Pour into a medium size saucepan and simmer over medium low heat for 20 minutes.

3. Serve hot.

Creamy Yukon Gold Potato Soup

SERVES: 3

INGREDIENTS:

2 tablespoons olive oil

1 cup Yukon Gold potatoes, peeled and cubed

¼ cup celery, sliced

½ cup onion, diced

2 tablespoons diced parsnips

1 teaspoon sea salt

1 cup water

1 vegetable bouillon cube (Morga)

2 cups nondairy milk of your choice

Dash freshly ground black pepper

DIRECTIONS:

1. In a large saucepan, heat the oil and sauté the potatoes, celery, onions, and parsnips over medium high heat for 7 to 8 minutes.

2. Add the salt, water, bouillon, nondairy milk, and pepper. Cover and cook over medium low heat for 25 to 30 minutes.

3. Serve hot.

Creamy Mushroom Soup

SERVES: 4

INGREDIENTS:

⅓ cup extra virgin olive oil

24 ounces mushrooms, sliced

2 large shallots, sliced

1½ pounds yellow onions, sliced

13.5-ounce can coconut milk

4 cups water

3 tablespoons fresh rosemary, chopped

2 teaspoons Himalayan sea salt

¾ teaspoon freshly ground black pepper

DIRECTIONS:

1. In a large saucepan sauté mushrooms, shallots, and onions in oil over medium high heat for 15 minutes.

2. Add coconut milk, water, rosemary, salt, and pepper. Cook an additional 10 minutes.

3. Process in a food processor or blender for 3 minutes.

4. Serve.

JOHN

I developed psoriatic arthritis 30 years ago. I underwent surgery to fuse my right wrist. My knees and neck were deteriorating, so I used heavy medications and over-the-counter analgesics. My blood pressure became elevated and I was advised to change careers. My daughter motivated me to join a health support group. Today, I am vegan and eat no sugar or wheat. After I began the protocol and juicing, I became pain-free in four weeks. I take no more medications, and all swelling subsided. My doctor commented that the condition of my knee joints is the best he has observed, and my blood pressure is normal. I am able to take long walks. I have reclaimed my life. Neighbors who have observed my improvement now follow the protocol. One couple, a diabetic and his wife who has multiple sclerosis, report physical improvements. By following the protocol, my cousin lost 10 lbs in two weeks and no longer has heartburn.

Cream of Sweet Potato Soup

MAKES: 2 quarts

INGREDIENTS:

2 cups cashews, soaked at least 1 hour in water

2 tablespoons unsalted nondairy butter

3 cloves garlic, minced

1 large onion, sliced thinly

1½ pounds sweet potatoes, chopped

4 cups low sodium vegetable broth

1 bunch fresh watercress

DIRECTIONS:

1. In a blender or Vitamix, add the soaked cashews, watercress, and 2 cups of water. Puree until smooth. Set aside.

2. In a large saucepan over medium heat melt butter. Sauté the garlic and onion until the garlic turns golden brown.

3. Add the sweet potatoes and 2 cups vegetable stock to the saucepan. Bring to a boil then reduce to a simmer for 20 minutes, until the potatoes are soft.

4. Add the watercress and cashew milk from blender to the potatoes and simmer for 5 minutes.

5. Remove saucepan from heat and puree soup in batches in a blender. Then return the soup to the saucepan.

6. Add more water to achieve desired consistency.

Note: This soup can be reheated if not allowed to boil. You may use homemade stock as long as it has not been made with vegetables that have high sodium content. You may use low sodium vegetable powder to be sure.

Mediterranean White Bean Soup

SERVES: 3

INGREDIENTS:

¼ cup olive oil

¾ cup yellow or white onions, chopped

3 cups fresh tomatoes, chopped

½ cup white mushrooms sliced

1 cup gluten-free farfalle pasta, cooked

¼ cup fresh parsley, chopped

1 cup white beans (canned), rinsed

2 teaspoons salt

½ teaspoon black pepper, freshly ground

2 cups water

⅛ teaspoon cayenne pepper

DIRECTIONS:

1. In a medium size saucepan, heat oil and sauté the onions and tomatoes over high heat for 5 minutes.

2. Add the remaining ingredients, reduce the heat to medium low, cover, and cook for an additional 20 minutes.

3. Serve immediately.

Papaya Yam Soup

SERVES: 2

INGREDIENTS:

2 to 3 yams (1¼ cups juice, ½ cup pulp)

2 papayas (1 cup juice)

2½ to 3 cups purified water

½ teaspoon nutmeg, ground

⅛ teaspoon cinnamon

½ teaspoon cardamom

¼ cup papaya sliced, as garnish (optional)

¼ cup fresh cherries or red grapes, as garnish (optional)

DIRECTIONS:

1. Separately push the yams and papayas through the juicer. Set aside 1¼ cups of the yam juice, ½ cup of the yam pulp, and 1 cup of the papaya juice.

2. In a medium size saucepan combine the juices, pulp, water, nutmeg, cinnamon, and cardamom. Bring to a boil over high heat, then remove and puree in blender.

3. Garnish with the papaya slices and red grapes.

4. Serve hot or cold.

DAMON

I felt frustrated and I could not muster up energy. I overslept, my hair was graying, my sinus infections drove me mad, and my cholesterol and blood pressure were elevated. This was not me, and I had to find a method of true reversal.

I went on Gary's protocol carefully. It was easy. I enjoyed new foods. I learned to understand body mechanisms. My elevated blood levels are normal now. My sinus problems are gone. I sleep less and awake with energy. My hair texture has improved and I have less graying. I am determined to achieve and have relationships with my family.

Sweet and Sour Lentil Soup

SERVES: 4

INGREDIENTS:

8 cups vegetable stock (see page 113)

2 cups apple juice

1 cup lentils

1 carrot sliced

1 large stalk celery, sliced

1 teaspoon garlic powder

1 teaspoon onion powder

2 teaspoons parsley flakes

2 tablespoons apple cider vinegar

1 tablespoon tamari, to taste

DIRECTIONS:

1. Combine the stock and apple juice in a medium size soup pot and bring to a boil.

2. Add lentils, carrot, celery, garlic powder, onion powder, and parsley. Again, bring to a boil. Then lower the heat and allow to simmer for 30 minutes.

3. Add vinegar and tamari. Add more seasoning to taste. Continue to simmer for about 20 minutes or until the lentils are soft.

4. Serve hot.

Tomato Potato Soup

SERVES: 2

INGREDIENTS:

9 ounces potatoes, chopped

3 tablespoons sesame oil

¼ teaspoon cumin

1 teaspoon basil

1 teaspoon sea salt

3 ounces tomato, chopped

6 ounces bell peppers, chopped

3 ounces scallions, chopped

DIRECTIONS:

1. Boil potatoes for approximately 15 minutes in 4 cups water.

2. Transfer potatoes and cooking water to a blender and add seasonings. Puree until smooth.

3. Return mixture to saucepan and set on stove again over low heat and add the chopped vegetables.

4. Cook for an additional 10 to 15 minutes.

If a fruit or vegetable is red, there's a good chance it is a cancer preventative food source.

Spicy Spinach and Avocado Soup

SERVES: 4

INGREDIENTS:

1 cucumber (½ cup cucumber juice)

2 cups spinach, washed and chopped

2 cups tomatoes, chopped

½ ripe avocado

½ teaspoon ginger, peeled and chopped

¼ cup flaxseed oil

¾ teaspoon garlic, minced

1 tablespoon lemon juice

1 teaspoon apple cider vinegar

1 teaspoon light sweet white miso

¼ teaspoon cayenne pepper

1 teaspoon chia or flaxseeds as garnish (optional)

DIRECTIONS:

1. Push cucumber through juicer and set aside ½ cup juice.

2. In a blender combine cucumber juice, spinach, tomatoes, avocado, ginger, flaxseed oil, garlic, lemon juice, cider vinegar, miso, and cayenne. Blend until smooth.

3. Chill for 1 to 2 hours.

4. Garnish with chia or flaxseeds, if desired.

5. Serve chilled.

Portobello Tofu Rice Soup

SERVES: 2

INGREDIENTS:

2 tablespoons olive oil

1 cup leeks or scallions, sliced

1 yellow onion, diced

2 cups baby Portobello mushrooms, sliced

1 cup zucchini, chopped

½ cup basmati-wild rice mix

2 teaspoons sea salt

1 teaspoon black pepper

⅛ teaspoon cayenne

5½ cups purified water

1 cup firm tofu, cubed

¼ cup crunchy sprouts

DIRECTIONS:

1. In a large saucepan over medium heat add oil and sauté the leeks or scallions, onions, mushrooms, zucchini, rice, salt, pepper, and cayenne for 5 minutes.

2. Add the water and tofu. Bring to a boil.

3. Reduce the heat to medium low and simmer, covered, for 30 minutes until done.

4. Garnish with sprouts, if desired.

5. Serve hot.

Oriental Vegetable Noodle Soup

SERVES: 6

INGREDIENTS:

1 tablespoon sesame oil

1 onion, sliced

1 carrot, sliced

1 small green pepper, sliced

1 stalk celery, sliced

6 cups low sodium vegetable stock

1 package brown rice noodles, uncooked

2 tablespoons tamari

2 cups broccoli florets

1 cup scallions, sliced

4 tablespoons miso

DIRECTIONS:

1. Heat the sesame oil in a medium soup pot. Add the onion, carrots, green pepper, and celery. Sauté until all the vegetables are tender, about 5 minutes.

2. Add the stock and the pasta. Bring to a boil and cook for 15 minutes, or until the pasta is almost cooked.

3. Add the tamari and broccoli and cook for 5 minutes longer. Then add scallions.

4. Remove about 1 cup of the liquid from the pot and dissolve the miso in it. Return the mixture to the rest of the soup and bring to a light boil.

5. Serve hot.

Vegetable Stock

MAKES: 2 quarts

INGREDIENTS:

4 cups of vegetable scraps (old, soft celery and carrots, onion skins, potato peelings, etc.)

1 bulb garlic, separated into cloves but not peeled

3 quarts water

DIRECTIONS:

1. Place everything in a large soup pot. Bring to a boil and simmer, covered, for an hour. Remove from heat and let stand until the stock is cool enough to handle.

2. Strain, leaving a clear broth. Discard the vegetables.

3. Refrigerate the stock until you are ready to use it, which should be within a week.

Note: To make low sodium vegetable stock, follow the instructions above but use only low sodium vegetables—no spinach, celery, radishes, or watercress.

Gazpacho

SERVES: 5-6

INGREDIENTS:

32 ounces tomato juice

2 green peppers, chopped

6 medium tomatoes, chopped

2 large onions, coarsely chopped

2 large cucumbers, coarsely chopped

2 pimientos (canned), drained

¼ teaspoon coarsely ground black pepper

4 teaspoons tamari (soy sauce)

²/₃ cup extra virgin olive oil

½ teaspoon Tabasco

²/₃ cup red wine vinegar

3 cloves garlic, minced

1 cup chopped scallions

DIRECTIONS:

1. In a large mixing bowl, combine 1 cup tomato juice with half the green pepper, ²/₃ of the tomatoes, half the onions, half of the cucumbers, and 1 pimiento.

2. Transfer to blender in batches and blend at high speed for about 1 minute. Put each of the remaining chopped vegetables in a separate dish, cover, and refrigerate.

3. Place the pureed vegetables in a large mixing bowl and add the remaining tomato juice, pepper, tamari, olive oil, Tabasco, and vinegar.

4. Chill, covered, in the refrigerator for at least 3 hours.

5. Stir the garlic into the soup just before serving. Mix well, preferably with a whisk. Sprinkle scallions on top.

6. Serve with the reserved chopped vegetables on the side of the plate or in separate bowls.

Chilled Cantaloupe Soup

SERVES: 2

INGREDIENTS:

1 teaspoon agar-agar flakes

1 cup orange or tangerine juice

1 tablespoon lemon juice

2 cups diced cantaloupe

Tofu sour cream, as garnish

DIRECTIONS:

1. Place agar-agar and orange juice in a small saucepan. Bring to a boil, reduce heat, and simmer until the agar-agar dissolves, about 10 minutes.

2. Place this mixture in a blender with the lemon juice and cantaloupe. Blend until pureed.

3. Chill in the refrigerator for at least 1 hour, preferably longer.

4. Just before serving, return the mixture to the blender for 1 to 2 minutes.

5. Serve with a spoonful of tofu sour cream on top.

Chilled Orange-Cucumber Mint Soup

SERVES: 6

INGREDIENTS:

2 oranges, peeled (1 cup juice)

1 cucumber (½ cup juice)

4 stalks celery (1 cup juice)

2 cups spring water

3 tablespoons palm or date sugar

1 cup plain rice yogurt

2 cucumbers, peeled and chopped

2 teaspoons fresh mint, finely chopped

6 tablespoons macadamia nut butter

2 teaspoons fresh parsley, chopped

¼ cup red grapes, as garnish

2 fresh figs, sliced as garnish

DIRECTIONS:

1. Juice the oranges, cucumber, and celery.

2. In a blender, combine the juices, spring water, palm or date sugar, rice yogurt, cucumbers, mint, macadamia nut butter, and parsley. Blend well.

3. Chill for 1 hour.

4. Garnish with the red grapes and fresh figs.

5. Serve cold.

Cold Cherry Soup

SERVES: 3-4

INGREDIENTS:

2 cups cherries, pitted and stemmed

¼ cup fresh lemon juice

1 cup strawberries, hulled

1 cup blueberries

1 tablespoon agar-agar

Cinnamon, to taste

1 orange, peeled and in wedges

DIRECTIONS:

1. Blend the cherries and lemon juice.

2. Add strawberries and blueberries. Blend until smooth.

3. Bring soup to a boil in a medium saucepan and dissolve agar agar for about 5 minutes.

4. Cool in refrigerator 30 minutes before serving.

5. Serve in a bowl with cinnamon garnish and orange wedges.

ANDREA
Participating in Gary Null's anti-aging program improved my health physically and emotionally. After I gave up dairy, sugar and fried foods, my allergies improved. I have fewer colds and better elimination. My energy increased, and I lost some weight. The behavior modification aspect of the program taught me to be more assertive and confident. I am closer to achieving my goals.

Fruit Soup

SERVES: 8

INGREDIENTS:

1 pound mixed dried fruit (apricots, apples, figs, prunes, peaches, etc.)

6 cups water

2½ cups apple juice

1 small cinnamon stick

2 medium apples, cored and cubed but not peeled

2 large pears, cored and cubed but not peeled

1 pint strawberries, hulled and sliced

2 tablespoons honey

3 tablespoons lemon juice

Nondairy yogurt or sour cream and fresh mint to garnish

DIRECTIONS:

1. Combine dried fruit, water, apple juice, and cinnamon stick in a large saucepan. Bring to a boil and allow to cook over medium heat for 30 minutes.

2. Add the apples and pears. Cook for an additional 3 minutes or until the apples and pears are just barely tender.

3. Add the strawberries and cook for an additional 2 minutes. Remove from the heat and stir in honey and lemon juice. Refrigerate until well chilled, 2 to 3 hours.

4. When serving, top with the yogurt or sour cream and a sprig of fresh mint, if desired.

Cold Strawberry Soup

SERVES: 2

INGREDIENTS:

1 pint strawberries, hulled

1 cup fruit juice (orange, papaya, apple-strawberry)

3 tablespoons lemon juice

2 tablespoons arrowroot

1 teaspoon honey

¾ cup nondairy sour cream

DIRECTIONS:

1. Place three quarters of the strawberries and the cup of fruit juice into a blender and puree. Pour the mixture into a saucepan.

2. Dissolve the arrowroot in the lemon juice and pour this mixture into the saucepan as well. Cook over medium heat until the mixture thickens, about 5 minutes. Remove from heat and add honey, if desired.

3. Slice the remaining strawberries and fold them, along with the sour cream, into the slightly cooled mixture. Refrigerate 2 to 3 hours until well chilled.

4. Serve cold with a teaspoon of sour cream on top.

Main Meals

Angel Hair with Radicchio 125
Spaghetti and Shiitake Saffron Tomato Sauce 127
Sesame Basil Spaghetti 128
Thai Peanut Rice Noodles 129
Ziti alla Pesto con Tomato 130
Quick Tomato Sauce 131
Mushroom and Onion Rice Pasta 133
Farfalle with Creamy Tomato Sauce 135
Walnut Tahini Pasta 137
Mushroom and Sweet Pea Spaghetti 139
Tofu With Miso Tahini Sauce 140
Miso Tahini Sauce 141
Veggie Pesto 142
Tarragon Tempeh 143
Toasted Sesame Tempeh 145
Wakame Stir Fry 147
Wild Rice with Spinach and Cream 148
Tomato Rice with Black Beans 149

Angel Hair with Radicchio

SERVES: 3-4

INGREDIENTS:

1 tablespoon extra-virgin olive oil

1 cup shiitake mushrooms, whole tops

1 cup black pitted olives, sliced

¾ teaspoon freshly ground black pepper

1 teaspoon sea salt

4 tablespoons capers

¼ cup fennel, chopped

1 cup soy or rice milk

1 tablespoon fresh basil, chopped

1 cup radicchio, sliced

1 cup fresh or frozen peas

1 cup nondairy Parmesan cheese

4 cups angel hair pasta, cooked

DIRECTIONS:

1. In a large saucepan, heat the oil over medium heat and sauté the mushrooms, olives, pepper, salt, capers, and fennel for 6 minutes.

2. Add milk, basil, radicchio, and peas. Cook for another 2 minutes.

3. Remove from heat and toss with the cheese and rice pasta.

Spaghetti and Shiitake Saffron Tomato Sauce

SERVES: 4

INGREDIENTS:

3 pounds plum tomatoes

1 pound rice spaghetti

¼ cup extra virgin olive oil

1 garlic bulb, peeled and minced

½ pound shiitake mushrooms, tops halved

2 teaspoons of saffron

2 teaspoons Himalayan sea salt

½ teaspoon black pepper

1½ ounces fresh basil, chopped

DIRECTIONS:

1. Fill a large saucepan with water and bring to a boil.

2. Mark an "X" on each tomato and cook in boiling water for 2 minutes until skins split open. Shock tomatoes in ice cold water and set aside.

3. Add spaghetti to boiling water and cook according to manufacturer directions.

4. Remove the tomato skins when cool enough to handle and dice small.

5. Add olive oil and minced garlic to a large saucepan and sauté on medium heat 4 minutes, until golden brown.

6. Add tomatoes, mushrooms, saffron, salt, and pepper to saucepan and cook for 7 to 10 minutes.

7. Remove sauce from heat and add basil.

8. Drain pasta and quick-rinse under running cold water.

9. Toss spaghetti with sauce and serve.

Sesame Basil Spaghetti

SERVES: 4

INGREDIENTS:

1 tablespoon extra-virgin olive oil

6 cloves garlic, minced

¼ cup raw sesame seeds

2 cups vegetable stock (see page 113)

¼ cup basil

6 tablespoons dry white wine

4 cups tomato sauce

1 pound quinoa spaghetti, uncooked

DIRECTIONS:

1. Heat the olive oil in a large saucepan. Add the garlic and sesame seeds and sauté until the garlic is golden brown.

2. Add the vegetable stock, basil, wine, and tomato sauce.

3. Mix well and cook for 20 to 30 minutes over medium-low heat.

4. Cook the spaghetti according to directions found on the package (do not add salt) and then drain.

5. Pour sauce over the spaghetti and toss lightly.

6. Serve immediately.

Thai Peanut Rice Noodles

SERVES: 2

INGREDIENTS:

7 tablespoons toasted sesame oil

1 clove garlic

¼ cup macadamia nut butter

½ tablespoon pure maple syrup

½ tablespoon fresh lime juice

⅓ cup plus 1 tablespoon water

¼ teaspoon hot chili oil or Tabasco sauce

½ cup scallions, sliced

1 cup shiitake mushrooms, stemmed and sliced

1 cup yellow onions, diced

¼ cup celery, diced

2 tablespoons Gomasio

¼ pound rice noodles, cooked

DIRECTIONS:

1. Combine 1 tablespoon oil, garlic, macadamia nut butter, maple syrup, lime juice, water, and hot chili oil in a blender and mix until smooth, about 2 to 3 minutes. Set aside.

2. In a large saucepan, heat remaining oil over medium heat, then sauté the scallions, mushrooms, onions, and celery for 8 to 10 minutes.

3. Remove from heat and stir in the Gomasio and peanut sauce from step 1.

4. Toss the rice noodles with the sauce in large bowl until all the noodles are covered.

5. Chill for an hour and a half.

6. Serve cold.

Ziti alla Pesto con Tomato

SERVES: 2-3

INGREDIENTS:

1 cup extra virgin olive oil

¼ cup +2 tablespoons fresh parsley, chopped

1¾ cup fresh basil

½ teaspoon freshly ground black pepper

1 teaspoon Himalayan salt

½ cup pine nuts, toasted

5 cups cooked ziti

2 cups chopped fresh tomatoes

1 large yellow pepper, diced

¾ cup black olives, sliced

DIRECTIONS:

1. To make pesto, place the oil, parsley, basil, pepper, and salt in a blender. Blend until smooth, about 3 to 4 minutes.

2. Toast pine nuts in hot sauté pan until golden, about 5 minutes over low heat.

3. Toss with the hot ziti with pesto, tomatoes, peppers, garlic, olives, and toasted pine nuts.

Quick Tomato Sauce

MAKES: 1½ cups

INGREDIENTS:

One 6-ounce can tomato paste
1½ cups Burgundy wine
4 cloves garlic, chopped
1 tablespoon fresh basil, chopped
2 teaspoons fresh oregano, chopped
1 tablespoon fresh parsley, chopped
2 teaspoons onion powder

DIRECTIONS:

1. Whisk all ingredients together in a small saucepan. Cook over medium-low heat for 10 minutes while whisking.

Mushroom and Onion Rice Pasta

SERVES: 2

INGREDIENTS:

3 ounces mushrooms, sliced

3 ounces onions, sliced

3 ounces fresh tomato, chopped

1 tablespoon basil

1 teaspoon oregano

½ teaspoon sea salt

2 tablespoons extra virgin olive oil

6 ounces rice pasta, cooked

DIRECTIONS:

1. In a large skillet, add olive oil and sauté mushrooms, onions, tomato, basil, oregano, and sea salt for 5 minutes.

2. Combine with rice pasta and toss gently.

3. Serve warm.

Members of the allium genus, such as onions, have anticancer properties. They also assist in the circulatory system and help to protect the liver.

Farfalle with Creamy Tomato Sauce

SERVES: 3-4

INGREDIENTS:

6 cups chopped fresh tomatoes

1 cup chopped fresh basil

2 teaspoons salt

1 cup coconut milk

2 cups sliced radicchio

2½ cups sliced mushrooms

1 cup chopped onions

1½ cups sliced broccoli florets

4 cloves garlic, chopped

½ teaspoon freshly ground black pepper

5 tablespoons extra virgin olive oil

6 cups cooked farfalle pasta

DIRECTIONS:

1. Cook all ingredients over medium-high heat for 10 minutes.

2. Serve over the hot pasta.

Tomatoes are a rich source of lycopene (a cancer-fighting nutrient) and antioxidants, as well as serving as an excellent example of an alkaline food. Alkaline foods help to balance out acid-forming foods by keeping the blood pH in its ideal range, which is important for the prevention and treatment of cancer. Ideally, the diet should consist of 80 percent alkaline-forming foods, such as those available from many raw fruits and vegetables, as well as nuts, seeds, grains, and legumes. The vast majority of Americans consume an excess of acid-forming foods, so it is especially important to make an effort to include alkaline-forming foods like tomatoes, strawberries, beets, asparagus, broccoli, bell peppers, carrots, and many others.

Walnut Tahini Pasta

SERVES: 4

INGREDIENTS:

2 tablespoons extra virgin olive oil

3 cloves garlic, minced

½ cup walnuts, chopped

2 tablespoons unsalted nondairy butter (Earth Balance)

½ cup tahini

½ cup lemon juice

1 cup water

4 cups quinoa elbow macaroni, cooked

½ cup tomato sauce

DIRECTIONS:

1. Heat the oil in a large saucepan. Add the garlic and walnuts. Cook until the garlic turns golden, stirring constantly.

2. Add the nondairy butter and the tahini, mixing well. Stir in the lemon juice. Add about ½ cup of water and mix well. Cook for approximately 5 minutes. Add remaining water.

3. Prepare pasta according to directions on package (but do not add salt).

4. Drain and add to the saucepan with tahini sauce. Simmer for 3 minutes.

5. Finish with tomato sauce.

Mushroom and Sweet Pea Spaghetti

SERVES: 2

INGREDIENTS:

1½ cups fresh sweet peas

⅓ cup extra virgin olive oil

One 8-ounce package mushrooms, sliced

2 cups tomato, chopped

¾ teaspoon sea salt

1 teaspoon fresh oregano

One 7.5-ounce package basil, chopped

One 10-ounce package rice spaghetti

DIRECTIONS:

1. Boil peas in 4 cups water for 15 minutes drain and set aside.

2. In a large skillet over medium-high heat add olive oil. Sauté the mushrooms with the tomatoes, salt, and oregano for 5–8 minutes.

3. Cook spaghetti according to instructions on the box.

4. Combine the rice spaghetti, peas, and basil with the mushroom and tomato mixture. Toss gently.

5. Serve immediately.

The portobello, oyster, reishi, and maitoki mushrooms are among approximately two hundred different varieties whose health-enhancing skills have been noted. Even the common white button mushroom is an excellent breast cancer chemopreventative agent.

Tofu With Miso Tahini Sauce

INGREDIENTS:

½ cup and ½ teaspoon sesame seeds

2 oranges, peeled, sliced, and seeded

1 tablespoon toasted sesame oil

1 cup oranges, juiced

¼ teaspoon orange extract

Pinch tamari

One 12-ounce package firm tofu

DIRECTIONS:

1. In large bowl, combine ½ cup sesame seeds, oranges, oil, orange juice, orange extract, and tamari. Mix well.

2. Place the tofu in the bowl and marinate for 1 hour in the refrigerator.

3. Remove the tofu from the marinade and broil about 8 to 10 minutes on each side.

4. Pour Miso Tahini sauce (see below) over the tofu and sprinkle with remaining sesame seeds.

5. Serve with short grain brown rice.

Miso Tahini Sauce

MAKES: 2 cups

INGREDIENTS:

¼ cup white miso paste

1 cup sesame tahini

¼ cup agave

2 tablespoons ginger juice

1 tablespoon umeboshi plum paste

2 teaspoons apple cider vinegar

DIRECTIONS:

1. Combine the above ingredients in a food processor fitted with a metal blade and process for 1–2 minutes.

Veggie Pesto

MAKES: 1 cup

INGREDIENTS:

¼ pound shelled walnuts

1½ cups fresh parsley

5 garlic cloves, peeled

1 cup extra virgin olive oil

¾ teaspoon salt

¼ teaspoon fresh ground black pepper

1½ teaspoons oregano

1½ teaspoons rosemary

1½ teaspoons thyme

3 teaspoons basil

¼ cup freshly grated nondairy Romano cheese

DIRECTIONS:

1. Chop the nuts and set aside.

2. Wash the parsley and pat dry with a towel. Remove stems.

3. Combine parsley and all other ingredients except for nuts and cheese in a blender and puree.

4. Remove from blender and transfer to a large mixing bowl.

5. Add nuts and cheese. Mix well.

6. Serve with soups, steamed vegetables, or salads.

Tarragon Tempeh

SERVES: 1

INGREDIENTS:

2 tablespoons safflower oil

3 ounces tempeh, cut into ½-inch pieces

1 ounce Brazil nuts, chopped

2 teaspoons fresh chives, minced

1 teaspoon tarragon

½ teaspoon salt

DIRECTIONS:

1. Preheat oven to 350°F.

2. Lightly grease baking sheet with 1 tablespoon oil and set aside.

3. In a large skillet, add remaining oil and sauté tempeh for 3 minutes, over medium heat. Set aside.

4. Blend Brazil nuts in a blender until finely ground.

5. Mix nut meal with chives, tarragon, salt, as well as 1 ounce water.

6. Toss the tempeh in the nut and herb mixture and place on baking sheet.

7. Place in oven and bake for 15 minutes.

8. Serve.

Toasted Sesame Tempeh

SERVES: 1

INGREDIENTS:

3 tablespoons macadamia nut oil

2 tablespoons toasted sesame seed oil

2 cups tempeh, cut into ½-inch pieces
(one 8-ounce package)

¼ cup pine nuts

3 tablespoons sesame seeds

2 teaspoons fresh chives, minced

1 tablespoon + 1 teaspoon fresh
tarragon, minced

1 teaspoon sea salt

2 tablespoons water

DIRECTIONS:

1. Preheat oven to 350°F.

2. Lightly grease baking sheet with macadamia nut oil.

3. In a heavy skillet, heat sesame oil and sauté tempeh for about 5 minutes over medium-high heat.

4. In a food processor, process pine nuts until finely ground, about 20 seconds.

5. Mix nut meal with sesame seeds, chives, tarragon, salt, and 1 ounce of water.

6. Stir together nut mixture with tempeh and place on a baking sheet. Bake for 15 minutes.

7. Serve immediately.

Wakame Stir Fry

SERVES: 2

INGREDIENTS:

1 pound extra firm tofu, ½-inch cubes

1 cup wakame sea vegetables, soaked and chopped

1 cup scallions, sliced

3 tablespoons toasted sesame oil

1 cup kabocha squash, ½-inch cubes, steamed

1 cup rice, cooked

2 tablespoons plus 1 teaspoon tamari sauce

1 cup fresh pineapple, diced

2 tablespoons black sesame seeds

1 tablespoon grated ginger

DIRECTIONS:

1. Saute tofu, wakame, and scallions over medium heat in sesame oil for 5 minutes.

2. In a mixing bowl, toss sauté ingredients with kabocha squash, rice, tamari, pineapple, sesame seeds, and grated ginger.

CHARLES

My journey toward improving my health began when I attended a Gary Null seminar. I worked in construction as an ironworker and had several accidents. During my younger years I held several jobs at a time and developed hypertension. It was time to rebuild my physical system. I considered my energy to be adequate for an aging man. I gradually investigated organic foods and vegetarian replacements for flesh foods. My health is maintained with supplements, lifting weights, gardening, and drinking power shakes with red and green powders. I still work in building and construction and just built a playhouse for my grandchildren. Listening to health programs on the radio gave me some information; however, following today 's healthier lifestyle and taking proper products supplies me with more energy than I have ever had. I bounce back easily from exhaustion. Except for a constant knee condition, I do not feel the consequences of falling off buildings. I do not have hypertension anymore. My family does not follow or cooper-ate with my food preparation. I prepare my meals separately and enjoy them. Hopefully, one day my grandchildren will open to this healthy concept. I feel younger than my sixty-nine years and look forward to a happy future.

Wild Rice with Spinach and Cream

SERVES: 2-3

INGREDIENTS:

2 cups cooked long grain rice

½ cup cooked wild rice

½ cup cooked chopped onion

1 cup sliced celery

1 cup sliced mushrooms

½ teaspoon sea salt

2 tablespoons chopped fresh thyme

3 tablespoons extra virgin olive oil

½ cup coconut milk

1 vegetable bouillon cube (Marga)

2 cups torn spinach

DIRECTIONS:

1. Sauté both rices with the onions, celery, mushrooms, sea salt, and thyme in the oil over medium heat until the onions are translucent.

2. Add coconut milk and vegetable bouillon cube and continue cooking for 5 minutes.

3. Add spinach and cook for 3 minutes.

4. Serve.

Tomato Rice with Black Beans

SERVES: 5

INGREDIENTS:

1 cup chopped onions

3 cups chopped fresh tomatoes

1½ cups frozen peas

6 tablespoons extra virgin olive oil

2 teaspoons sea salt

¼ teaspoon freshly ground black pepper

1½ tablespoons turmeric

15 ounces canned black beans

5½ cups short grain brown or wild rice blend, cooked

DIRECTIONS:

1. In a large saucepan combine the onions, tomatoes, peas, oil, sea salt, and pepper. Cook over medium high heat, covered, for 5 minutes until it thickens.

2. Stir in the turmeric, beans, and rice and heat through 5 minutes.

3. Serve.

Peanut Thai Rice Sauté

SERVES: 2

INGREDIENTS:

2 tablespoons peanut oil

1 cup zucchini, diced

1 cup chopped green onions

4 teaspoons chopped shallots

½ cup chopped unsalted roasted peanuts

3 cups cooked long grain brown rice

1 tablespoon chopped garlic

1 teaspoon sea salt

1 teaspoon freshly ground black pepper

½ cup chopped fresh arugula

4½ teaspoons chopped fresh mint, for garnish

DIRECTIONS:

1. Heat the peanut oil in a skillet or wok until hot, but not smoking, over high heat.

2. Add the zucchini, onions, shallots, peanuts, rice, garlic, salt, and pepper.

3. Sauté over medium high heat for 5 minutes.

4. Remove from heat then toss in arugula.

5. Garnish with chopped mint.

Oriental Golden Rice with Tofu

SERVES: 2

INGREDIENTS:

3 tablespoons extra virgin olive oil

2 large garlic cloves, minced

1 scallion, chopped

1 tablespoon onion, minced

1 teaspoon sea salt

¾ cup coconut milk

2 curry or bay leaves

1 tablespoon peeled and minced ginger

½ teaspoon turmeric

One 14-ounce package firm tofu, 1-inch cubes

½ teaspoon saffron

1½ cups rice

4 cups water

3 tablespoons cilantro, minced

2 teaspoon toasted sesame seeds

DIRECTIONS:

1. To cook rice, combine 1½ cups rice and water in medium saucepan, covered, over moderate heat.

2. In a large saucepan over medium heat add olive oil and sauté garlic, scallion, and onion with salt until onion is translucent, about 5 to 6 minutes.

3. Add coconut milk, curry or bay leaves, ginger, turmeric, tofu, and saffron. Cook for 10 minutes.

4. Add rice, cilantro, and sesame seeds. Cook uncovered for 10 minutes.

5. Serve warm.

Basmati Rice with Peppers and Fresh Herbs

SERVES: 2

INGREDIENTS:

1½ cups cooked brown basmati rice

¾ tablespoons chopped fresh marjoram

2 teaspoons chopped fresh tarragon

4 tablespoons small-diced red bell pepper

4 tablespoons small-diced yellow bell pepper

1 tablespoon cumin powder

½ teaspoon sea salt

¼ teaspoon freshly ground black pepper

3 tablespoons coconut oil

DIRECTIONS:

1. In a large saucepan combine all the ingredients and sauté over medium heat in the oil for 10 minutes.

2. Serve.

ANDREA

I weighed 300 pounds and wore size 24–26 clothing. I was not diagnosed with illnesses, but I felt exhausted, had painful varicose veins, back problems, was nauseated after meals, lactose intolerant, and had bad digestion. I ate flesh foods and dairy. I listened to *Natural Living* [radio show] and joined a support group.

Today I weigh 225 pounds and wear a size 18. I developed a sense of value in the group and can say "no." I feel centered and empowered. I juice and take supplements. By discovering a new world of health food stores, I choose products carefully. As a creative cook, I enjoy translating old recipes into vegan meals using grains. I am creating a dance area at home and enjoy biking, skiing, kayak class, and swimming lessons.

Mushroom and Pea Biryani

SERVES: 2

INGREDIENTS:

1½ cups brown basmati rice

4 cups water

1 cup fresh or frozen peas

1 large yellow onion, chopped (2 cups)

3 cups sliced shiitake mushrooms,
  de-stemmed

1 bay leaf

1½ teaspoons salt

¼ teaspoon freshly ground black pepper

3 tablespoons extra virgin olive oil

¼ teaspoon ground cardamom

1 teaspoon ground coriander

½ teaspoon ground ginger

½ teaspoon ground nutmeg

1 cinnamon stick

DIRECTIONS:

1. Cook 1½ cups brown basmati rice in 4 cups water, covered, on low heat for 40 minutes; set aside.

2. In a large saucepan sauté the peas, onions, and mushrooms with the bay leaf, salt, and pepper in the oil over medium high heat, until onions are translucent.

3. Drain any excess water the mushrooms may have thrown off. Stir in the rice and cardamom, coriander, ginger, nutmeg, and cinnamon stick. Cook until hot over medium heat.

4. Remove cinnamon stick before serving.

Risotto with Shiitake Mushrooms Parmesan

SERVES: 2

INGREDIENTS:

3½ cups coconut milk

1 cup stemmed and sliced shiitake mushrooms

1 cup Arborio rice, uncooked

1 tablespoon finely chopped fresh Italian parsley

¼ cup grated vegan Parmesan cheese

½ teaspoon Himalayan pink salt

¼ teaspoon freshly ground black pepper

DIRECTIONS:

1. In a saucepan bring the coconut milk to a simmer over low heat, being careful not to boil.

2. Stir in the mushrooms and rice and cook for 25 minutes or until creamy.

3. Add the remaining ingredients and cook an additional 2 minutes over a low flame.

4. Serve hot.

Shiitake mushrooms have a particular polysaccharide complex sugar that appears to have some powerful antitumor and antimutagenic qualities. For this reason, the Japanese are taking a close look at the genus Agaricus, which includes the ordinary mushroom found in the grocery store. It is not yet known whether this mushroom's activity even approaches that of the better-known medicinal mushrooms, but it does appear to have health-promoting properties such as combating the effects of free radicals. An extract of the shiitake mushroom, lentinan, serves as an immune modulator and can help reduce the side effects of chemotherapy.

Curried Chick Peas with Veggies

SERVES: 2

INGREDIENTS:

1 cup turnips, cut in ¼-inch thick pieces

One half pound broccoli florets, cut into bite size pieces

One 15-ounce can garbanzo beans

1 cup barley

2 tablespoons fresh chives, minced

2 tablespoons toasted sesame oil

2 teaspoons curry powder

3 tablespoons lemon juice

1 teaspoon sea salt

DIRECTIONS:

1. To cook barley, combine with 5 cups water in a small saucepan and cook covered over moderate heat for 25 to 30 minutes.

2. Steam turnips and broccoli for 8 to 10 minutes

3. Toss together in a large mixing bowl with remaining ingredients and mix until well combined.

4. Serve warm.

Grandma's Stuffed Cabbage

SERVES: 4

INGREDIENTS:

1 medium white cabbage
3 cups brown rice, cooked
1 cup mushrooms, chopped
1 teaspoon garlic powder
1 teaspoon oregano

1 teaspoon basil
16 ounces tomato sauce
Nondairy Romano or Parmesan cheese (optional)

DIRECTIONS:

1. Preheat oven to 375°F.

2. Parboil the cabbage for about 5 minutes by placing it in a large pot of boiling water. After draining, remove the core of the cabbage and you will find each leaf comes off easily.

3. While the cabbage is cooling, combine the brown rice, chopped mushrooms, and seasonings in a separate bowl.

4. When the leaves are cool enough to handle, place approximately 3 tablespoons of the mixture on one leaf, then fold up carefully, tucking in the sides as you roll. Use 2 smaller leaves together to make the last rolls.

5. Place the rolls seam side down, in a shallow pan and spoon the tomato sauce over. If desired, sprinkle some nondairy Romano or Parmesan cheese over the top.

6. Bake for 40 minutes or until thoroughly heated.

Baby Lima Bean and Mushroom Sauté

SERVES: 2

INGREDIENTS:

2 tablespoons extra virgin olive oil

1 cup oyster mushrooms, sliced

½ cup onions, sliced

1 teaspoon sea salt

1 teaspoon garlic, minced

1 tablespoon fresh parsley, chopped

1 cup lima beans, cooked

1 cup millet, cooked

DIRECTIONS:

1. In a skillet, heat oil and sauté mushrooms and onions until onions are translucent.

2. Add sea salt, garlic, parsley, lima beans, and millet.

3. Mix well and serve warm.

VIOLA

I was afraid and confused. I was overweight and stuck in an unhealthy home situation. The hours stuck in self doubt left me with a fear of being crazy. There was no one to talk to and nowhere to turn. At first I felt [when I joined a Null self help group and heard about the dietary changes that were being advocated] "How can I give up all the food I ate my whole life?" Then I remembered how stuck I was, so I vowed to go on Gary Null's program totally. I lost weight and became a vegetarian.

My children and I thrive on the program. I will not ever again tolerate verbal abuse. I set firm boundaries. My children and I recently moved to another state and now we have a peaceful home. Uncluttering the past brought new friends into our lives.

Mushroom and Tofu Sautéed in Miso

SERVES: 3-4

INGREDIENTS:

2 tablespoons sesame or olive oil

14 ounces extra firm tofu, cut into ½-inch cubes

½ pound mushrooms, cut in thick slices

4 tablespoons brown rice miso

1 teaspoon maple syrup

1 tablespoon tamari

1 teaspoon powdered ginger

½ cup parsley, chopped

3 cups brown rice, cooked

DIRECTIONS:

1. Heat the oil over medium-high heat in a large skillet or wok. Add the tofu and mushrooms and sauté 3 minutes.

2. Combine the miso, maple syrup, tamari, and ginger in a small bowl. Make sure the miso is well mixed.

3. Add this mixture to the mushrooms and tofu and sauté for 5 minutes.

4. Remove from heat and mix in parsley.

5. Serve hot with brown rice.

Mushroom Cream Hijiki

MAKES: 1 quart

INGREDIENTS:

¼ cup safflower oil

1½ pounds assorted mushrooms, ½ pound sliced

½ pound Spanish onions, sliced

¼ cup Earth Balance nondairy butter spread

¼ cup gluten free flour

1 cup hijiki, soaked

3 cups hemp milk

2 tablespoons tamari

DIRECTIONS:

1. In a large saucepan, heat the oil and sauté the mushrooms and onions briefly.

2. Add the butter. After it has melted, whisk in the flour. Cook over low heat, stirring, until thickened, about 5 minutes.

3. Prepare hijiki by soaking it in warm water 20 minutes. Drain. Cut into ½-inch strips. Add the hijiki to the mushrooms and onions.

4. Heat the hemp milk and the tamari in a large saucepan. Add the mushrooms-flour-hijiki mixture and stir over low heat until thickening takes place.

5. To refrigerate the sauce, cool at room temperature with a cover off or it will sour.

Oriental Quinoa with Purple Cabbage

SERVES: 2

INGREDIENTS:

½ cup sliced red bell peppers

1½ cups sliced purple cabbage

½ cup Brussels sprouts, quartered

3 tablespoons toasted sesame oil

3 tablespoons tamari

2 tablespoons gomasio

1 cup cooked quinoa

2 tablespoons chopped fresh parsley

⅛ teaspoon cayenne pepper

DIRECTIONS:

1. In a medium size saucepan sauté the peppers, cabbage, and sprouts in the oil over medium heat for 5 minutes.

2. Add the remaining ingredients and mix well. Cook an additional 3 minutes.

Ratatouille Supreme

SERVES: 4-6

INGREDIENTS:

1 pound zucchini, ½-inch cubes

1 small eggplant, ½-inch cubes, about 1 pound

1 yellow onion, sliced

½ cup extra virgin olive oil

4 large cloves garlic, minced

2 pounds tomato, chopped

1 green pepper, chopped

1¼ teaspoons sea salt

¼ teaspoon freshly ground pepper

1½ teaspoons basil

1 teaspoon thyme

DIRECTIONS:

1. In a large skillet over moderate heat, sauté the zucchini, eggplant, and onion in the olive oil for about 10 minutes, or until the onion is translucent.

2. Stir in the garlic, tomatoes, green peppers, sea salt, black pepper, basil, and thyme. Cook covered over medium heat for 10 to 15 minutes, or until vegetables are tender.

3. Serve immediately over brown rice or any other grain.

Garlic not only stimulates the immune system but also serves as an antibacterial, antiviral, and antifungal element. Garlic is a mild natural antibiotic that increases the activity of natural killer cells so that they can better fight off viruses and tumor cells. It also works actively to fight off infections.

Stewed Green Cabbage with Corn and Peas

SERVES: 2

INGREDIENTS:

5 cups shredded green cabbage, about 2 pounds

2 cups water

¼ cup diced onions

¼ teaspoon caraway seeds

1 teaspoon salt

$\frac{1}{8}$ teaspoon freshly ground black pepper

½ cup frozen peas

½ cup frozen corn

2 teaspoons curry powder

2 tablespoons extra virgin olive oil

DIRECTIONS:

1. In a medium sized saucepan combine all the ingredients and bring to a boil.

2. Reduce the heat to medium high and cook for an additional 15 minutes. Stirring occasionally.

3. Serve hot or cold.

Cruciferous vegetables like cabbage and kale are good sources of cancer preventing phytonutrients. Cabbage is high in carotenoids and other antioxidants that guard against heart disease, cancer, and problems in blood sugar regulation. Cabbage also contains manifold glutamine, an amino acid that contributes to the anti-inflammatory activities in the body. This acid protects from infectious complications due to human papilloma virus (HPV). Compounds in cabbage juice have been observed to have favorable effects on stomach and colorectal cancer; cabbage juice will even quicken the healing of peptic ulcers.

Sweet and Sour Tempeh

SERVES: 2

INGREDIENTS:

2 cups tempeh, cubed

3 tablespoons coconut oil

2 cups pineapple, cubed

2 cups broccoli florets, steamed

2 large red peppers, seeded and diced

2 teaspoons chopped garlic

¾ cup sliced scallion

½ cup unsalted roasted peanuts, chopped

SAUCE:

1 tablespoon tomato paste

1 tablespoon tamari

2 tablespoons maple syrup

9 tablespoons lime or lemon juice

¼ teaspoon hot sauce

DIRECTIONS:

1. In a skillet, brown tempeh in coconut oil over medium heat for 3 minutes then add pineapple, broccoli, peppers, and garlic and sauté 2 more minutes.

2. Reduce heat to low.

3. Whisk together the sauce ingredients in a small bowl.

4. Add the sauce to the skillet and sauté 2 minutes on high.

5. Remove from heat and toss in scallions. Garnish with peanuts.

Peperonata

SERVES: 6

INGREDIENTS:

½ cup extra virgin olive oil

1 large onion, chopped

3 cloves garlic, thinly sliced

4 bay leaves

6 green peppers, chopped

6 tomatoes, quartered

1 tablespoon basil, chopped

½ tablespoon oregano leaves

1 teaspoon sea salt

DIRECTIONS:

1. Heat the olive oil in a large skillet over medium heat. Add the onion, garlic, and bay leaves and sauté until the onion is golden brown.

2. Add green peppers and cook for almost 10 minutes, until the pepper changes color, stirring constantly.

3. Add tomatoes and seasonings. Lower the heat and simmer gently for 10 to 15 minutes.

4. Remove bay leaves.

5. Serve warm.

Pyramid Pea Casserole

SERVES: 2

INGREDIENTS:

3 ounces chickpeas, cooked

3 ounces barley, cooked

3 ounces turnip greens, chopped

1½ ounces Brazil nuts, chopped

2 tablespoons extra virgin olive oil

2 teaspoons chopped fresh chives

¼ teaspoon thyme

½ teaspoon curry

½ teaspoon sea salt

DIRECTIONS:

1. Preheat oven to 375°F.

2. Lightly grease a 4 x 8 baking pan with olive oil.

3. Combine all ingredients and mix well.

4. Transfer to baking pan and bake for 25 minutes.

Tofu Marsala

SERVES: 2

INGREDIENTS:

1 block firm tofu (14 ounce) sliced into
  1½-inch slices

1 cup coconut flour for dredging + 1
  tablespoon for the sauce

2 tablespoons parsley, chopped

½ cup extra virgin olive oil

1 tablespoon fresh garlic, minced

¾ pounds portobello mushrooms
  coarsely chopped

2 cups marsala wine

½ teaspoon sea salt

½ teaspoon lemon pepper or freshly
  ground black pepper

DIRECTIONS:

1. Dredge the tofu in coconut flour and 1 tablespoon parsley.

2. In a large skillet, warm ¼ cup olive oil over medium heat. Add tofu and sauté 3 to 5 minutes on each side until golden brown. Remove tofu from pan and clean plan.

3. In the same pan, sauté garlic and mushrooms in remaining oil for 5 minutes.

4. Add wine into the pan and deglaze. Reduce heat to low and stir 1 tablespoon of flour into the wine.

5. Return the tofu to the pan, turning the coat with the sauce. Add salt and pepper.

6. Remove from pan and sprinkle with remaining parsley.

7. Serve.

Tofu Portobello Burger

SERVES: 1

INGREDIENTS:

3 medium Portobello mushroom tops

2 teaspoon extra virgin olive oil

2 teaspoons toasted sesame oil

3 cloves garlic, sliced

1 onion, sliced very thin

9 pieces of tempeh bacon

1 large bun, pan grilled, or 1 to 2 slices Ezekiel bread, toasted or pan heated with Earth Balance spread

1 tomato slice

1 leaf romaine lettuce or salad vegetables

Vegan mayonnaise

Organic mustard sweetened with agave

DIRECTIONS:

1. Sauté mushrooms over medium-high heat in olive oil for 10 minutes.

2. Add sesame oil, garlic, and onion and sauté for 5 minutes.

3. Sauté tempeh bacon in 3 tablespoons of olive oil until crispy.

4. Remove mushrooms and add tempeh bacon and cook for 3 minutes each side.

5. Place each item on bun and dress with condiments to taste.

6. Serve immediately.

Tomatoes Stuffed with Spinach and Cheese

SERVES: 6

INGREDIENTS:

6 medium tomatoes

Sea salt, to taste

10 ounces fresh spinach, washed very
well and drained

¼ cup nondairy Parmesan cheese,
grated

1 cup nondairy ricotta cheese

2 tablespoons egg replacer

1 teaspoon sea salt

⅛ teaspoon grated nutmeg

½ teaspoon freshly ground black pepper

2 tablespoon unsalted nondairy butter
(Earth Balance), softened

DIRECTIONS:

1. Preheat oven to 350°F.

2. Cut a ½ inch slice from the stem of each tomato, scoop out the pulp and seeds and save for another use.

3. Stand tomatoes upside down on paper towels and set aside for at least 30 minutes or until ready to stuff.

4. Tear the spinach into pieces. Place the spinach, the two cheeses, the egg replacer, salt, nutmeg, black pepper, and butter in a large mixing bowl and mix well.

5. Stuff the tomatoes with the spinach and cheese mixture. Place the tomatoes in a well-greased baking dish. Bake for about 30 minutes, or until the top is browned and they are heated through.

6. Serve hot or at room temperature.

Maple Glaze

MAKES: ¾ cup

INGREDIENTS:

½ cup apricot preserves
¼ cup pure maple syrup
1 teaspoon almond or lemon extract

DIRECTIONS:

1. Whisk all ingredients together in a small saucepan over low heat for 5 minutes.

2. Pour over cakes or doughnuts. It also makes for a great glaze for tempeh and tofu.

Tangy Orange Sauce

MAKES: 1 cup

INGREDIENTS:

2 oranges, peeled and segmented

½ cup orange juice

1 teaspoon ground ginger

¼ cup pure maple syrup

DIRECTIONS:

1. Combine all the ingredients in a saucepan and bring to a simmer over medium high heat.

2. Cook for 5 minutes and serve hot. It is best over nondairy ice cream and type of kebob (fish, tempeh).

Orange-Maple Cream Sauce

MAKES: ¾ cup

INGREDIENTS:

1 cup rice milk

2 teaspoons orange extract

2 tablespoons pure maple syrup

3 tablespoons egg replacer

¼ teaspoon ground nutmeg

DIRECTIONS:

1. In a small saucepan combine all the ingredients and mix well with a whisk.

2. Heat slowly over medium heat till thick, stirring constantly with a spoon to prevent lumping and burning.

3. Serve chilled or warm over bread pudding or any type of sweet bread.

Desserts

Baked Apple Fruit Medley

SERVES: 4

INGREDIENTS:

4 large baking apples (Rome Beauty)

1 cup small-diced dried figs

½ cup small-diced dates

1 medium Bartlett pear, peeled and minced

¼ cup chopped walnuts

½ cup diced orange sections (remove seeds before dicing)

4 teaspoons date syrup

¼ teaspoon cinnamon

4 tablespoons Earth Balance nondairy butter, melted

DIRECTIONS:

1. Core the apples and enlarge the core hole for the filling.

2. Slice apples horizontally into ½ inch rings and arrange on a baking sheet.

3. In a medium mixing bowl, combine all the remaining ingredients except the butter. Mix until combined.

4. Stuff the apple centers with the mixture.

5. Preheat oven to 375°F.

6. Drizzle butter atop the apple rings and bake for 20 minutes.

7. Serve warm or chilled.

Pineapple Tapioca Pudding

SERVES: 2

INGREDIENTS:

2½ cups coconut milk

½ cup small tapioca granules

1 teaspoon vanilla extract

3 tablespoons pure maple syrup

½ cup crushed pineapple, drained

DIRECTIONS:

1. In a medium-size saucepan over low heat, bring the milk, tapioca, vanilla, and syrup to a simmer.

2. Cook about 7 minutes or until thickened.

3. Stir in the pineapple and chill for 2 hours.

Sweet Raspberry-Blueberry Crumble

SERVES: 2

INGREDIENTS:

½ cup rice flour

¼ cup gluten free flour

1 tablespoon arrowroot

¾ cup coconut palm sugar

3 ounces Earth Balance buttery spread, melted

½ cup blueberries, fresh or frozen

½ raspberries, fresh or frozen

1 tablespoon lemon juice, freshly squeezed

¼ cup maple syrup or other sweetener

¼ teaspoon cinnamon

2 dollops whipped nondairy cream for topping (see note)

DIRECTIONS:

1. Preheat oven to 300°F.

2. In a large bowl combine flour, arrowroot, and coconut palm sugar.

3. Add melted buttery spread and mix with pastry blender until mixture resembles bread crumbs.

4. In a soufflé dish combine blueberries and raspberries. Sprinkle with lemon juice, maple syrup, and cinnamon.

5. Cover berries evenly with the crumble topping, pressing down gently.

6. Bake for 17 to 23 minutes, or until topping is golden brown.

7. Top with whipped nondairy cream sweetened with berries and maple syrup.

8. Serve hot or cold.

Note: For a special treat, drizzle with melted dark chocolate or heated raspberry jam.

Poached Pears with Raspberry Sauce

SERVES: 8

INGREDIENTS:

4 pears, peeled and halved

2 cups apple juice

1 teaspoon lemon extract

2 cups fresh or frozen raspberries

¾ cup maple sugar

4 fresh mint leaves for garnish

DIRECTIONS:

1. In a large saucepan, bring the pears, juice, and extract to a boil. Reduce to low and cook for 10 minutes, covered.

2. In a separate saucepan, combine the raspberries and sugar. Bring to a simmer and let cook for 2 minutes.

3. Remove from heat and serve over the drained pears.

4. Garnish with the mint leaves. Excellent with vanilla ice cream or Rice Dream.

Banana Pudding

SERVES: 6-8

INGREDIENTS:

2 cups fresh blueberries

2 bananas, peeled

4 figs, chopped

2 nectarines, pitted and sliced

1 cup plain nondairy yogurt

2 tablespoons chopped almonds

DIRECTIONS:

1. In a food processor, puree the blueberries, bananas, and figs until you have a smooth texture.

2. Transfer the mixture to a shallow baking pan.

3. Arrange the nectarine slices on top of the blueberry mixture.

4. Spread the yogurt on top of the nectarines slices.

5. Sprinkle with almonds and serve.

Caramel Sauce

MAKES: ½ cup

INGREDIENTS:

1 cup date or maple sugar

¼ cup water

2 teaspoons almond extract

DIRECTIONS:

1. In a small saucepan, whisk ingredients together over low heat until the sugar dissolves.

2. Serve over puddings, cakes, and other sweets.

Almond Corn Crispies

MAKES: 12 bars

INGREDIENTS:

½ cup rice syrup

1½ teaspoons almond or lemon extract

2 tablespoons coconut oil

¼ cup almond butter

2 cups cereal flakes

¾ cup shredded unsweetened coconut

½ cup raisins

DIRECTIONS:

1. In a large saucepan heat syrup, extract, oil, and almond butter over medium heat for 2 to 3 minutes, mixing well.

2. Stir in the remaining ingredients, and then press into a greased 12 x 17-inch baking dish. Refrigerate for at least 15 minutes to set.

3. Cut into bars and serve.

Carob-Coated Macadamia Butter Balls

MAKES: 12 candies

INGREDIENTS:

½ cup macadamia nut butter

¼ cup maple sugar

¼ teaspoon lemon extract

1 cup unsalted roasted macadamia nuts, chopped

CAROB FROSTING:

¾ cup carob chips

¼ cup soy milk

¼ cup pure maple syrup

1 teaspoon vanilla extract

DIRECTIONS:

1. To make the Carob Frosting, melt the chips in the milk on low heat until fully melted. Using a whisk, mix in the syrup and vanilla and cook until creamy. Remove from the heat and set aside.

2. In a small bowl, cream together the macadamia nut butter, maple sugar, and extract.

3. Roll the mixture into small balls, coat with the Carob Frosting, and then roll in the macadamia nuts.

Note: Reheat carob frosting if it becomes too cold to handle effectively.

Carob-Coated Nut Bananas

MAKES: 10 bananas

INGREDIENTS:

½ cup rice syrup

1 teaspoon vanilla extract

1 cup carob chips

½ cup water

3 cups chopped unsalted roasted peanuts

10 bananas, peeled, frozen and skewered lengthwise with sticks

DIRECTIONS:

1. Combine the syrup, vanilla, chips, and water in a medium-size saucepan and cook over medium heat, stirring consistently, until chips dissolve.

2. Remove from heat and cool for 10 minutes for easier handling.

3. Roll the frozen bananas in the mixture and then the nuts.

4. Place on wax paper and freeze for 1 hour.

CATHY

I was bedridden for two weeks with Epstein-Barr disease and could not walk more than three minutes at a time. I lost some of my memory. I returned to work but only put in five hours a day, and went to bed as soon as I returned home. Stair climbing was difficult. My physician could do no more and suggested I do independent research. A homeopathic examination revealed food sensitivities. The day I watched Gary on PBS changed my life. I donated to the station and soon joined a support group. Today I carefully follow the protocol. I gave up chocolate without difficulty. At first the new food choices were difficult to accept, but today I am vegan and feel 1,000 percent better. I work seven hours a day and exercise after work. I walk one and a half hours and am training to race walk in the New York Marathon. I still need eight hours of sleep, possibly because of Epstein Barr, but my waking hours are productive. With a clear mind, good memory, energy, and concentration, I plan future occupations in art and volunteer work.

Cinnamon Papaya Pudding

SERVES: 2

INGREDIENTS:

3 ounces papaya

3 ounces oatmeal, cooked

6 ounces apple juice

3 tablespoons yacon syrup

2 tablespoons Ener-G Egg Replacer

¼ teaspoon cinnamon

3 ounces apples, cut into ½-inch cubes

DIRECTIONS:

1. Combine all ingredients in a blender except apples. Puree until smooth.

2. Transfer to saucepan and cook over medium heat for about 5 minutes.

3. Add apples and stir.

4. Chill in refrigerator for 45 minutes or until set.

5. Serve chilled.

Delightful Papaya Mousse

SERVES: 2

INGREDIENTS:

½ cup sliced avocado

¾ cup sliced papaya

1 tablespoon fresh lemon juice

2 tablespoons orange juice

½ teaspoon ground nutmeg

2 tablespoons Manuka honey

1 cup halved strawberries, as garnish

Fresh mint leaves, as garnish

DIRECTIONS:

1. Place the avocado, papaya, juices, nutmeg, and honey in a blender or food processor and blend until smooth.

2. Pour into small pudding dishes and chill 2 hours.

3. Serve garnished with the strawberries and mint.

Raspberry Mousse

SERVES: 2-4

INGREDIENTS:

1 cup raspberries fresh or frozen

1 cup exotic super foods young thai coconut meat, thawed

1 cup raw cashews, soaked overnight or at least for three hours, drained

2 tablespoons raw agave

1½ teaspoons fresh lemon juice

1½ teaspoons pure vanilla water (see page 213)

DIRECTIONS:

1. Add all ingredients to a food processor and process for 2 minutes. Transfer to a Vitamix and blend until smooth, about 2 minutes.

2. Serve in parfait cups or between cookies.

Peach Julep Pudding

SERVES: 2

INGREDIENTS:

6 ounces peaches, sliced

3 ounces barley, cooked

8 ounces peach juice

4 ounces organic honey

1½ ounces walnuts

1 teaspoon vanilla extract

2 teaspoons fresh mint

1 teaspoon lemon juice

DIRECTIONS:

1. Place all ingredients in blender. Puree until smooth.

2. Transfer to saucepan and whisk over medium heat for 5 minutes.

3. Chill for 45 minutes in refrigerator.

FATIMAH

I was a sugar addict and ate two pounds of it per day, creating a sick, uncomfortable body. I over-ate using junk food. My energy was low, my skin was bad, and my blood pressure and cholesterol were high. This inability to control myself stressed me. As I listened to Gary, I thought about freeing myself from these habits. I joined a support group.

It is wonderful to be free of compulsive eating. I lost 50 pounds. I do not crave sugar. My cholesterol and blood pressure are lower, and I have real, vital energy. Problem solving comes easily, my marriage is happier, and I meditate. The foods I eat are healthy and so is my outlook.

Mango Mousse

INGREDIENTS:

½ cup sliced avocado
¾ cup sliced mango
1 tablespoon fresh lemon juice
2 tablespoons orange juice
½ teaspoon ground nutmeg
2 tablespoons Manuka honey
1 cup halved strawberries, as garnish
Fresh mint leaves as garnish

DIRECTIONS:

1. Place the avocado, mango, juices, nutmeg, and honey in a blender or food processor and blend until smooth.

2. Pour into small pudding dishes and chill for two hours.

3. Serve garnished with the strawberries and mint.

Sunny Rice Pudding

SERVES: 2

INGREDIENTS:

3 ounces mango

3 ounces brown rice, cooked

5 teaspoons carob powder

1½ ounces sunflower seeds

1 ounce date sugar

1 teaspoon vanilla

1½ ounces dates

3 teaspoons Ener-G Egg Replacer

1 cup hemp milk

DIRECTIONS:

1. Combine all ingredients and puree until smooth.

2. Transfer to saucepan and cook over medium heat for 5 minutes, stirring frequently.

3. Chill in refrigerator for 45 minutes.

Sweet Crème Tofu

SERVES: 4

INGREDIENTS:

One 15-ounce package extra firm tofu
1 teaspoon lemon extract
½ cup pure maple syrup

DIRECTIONS:

1. Blend all the ingredients for 1 minute.

2. Chill in refrigerator at least 30 minutes before serving and serve chilled.

Raisin Oatmeal Cookies

MAKES: 13 cookies (3 oz. each)

INGREDIENTS:

1 cup Earth Balance Soy Butter, softened

1 cup pure maple syrup

4½ teaspoons vanilla extract

1½ cups gluten free flour

½ teaspoon baking powder

2 cups rolled oats

½ cup raisins

½ cup chopped pecans

½ cup chopped roasted macadamia nuts

DIRECTIONS:

1. In a medium size bowl, use a whisk to cream together the butter, syrup, and vanilla.

2. Whisk together the flour and baking powder, and then add to the butter mixture with the oats and combine.

3. Stir in the remaining ingredients.

4. Refrigerate the dough for 3 hours. Roll into balls and press out onto a greased cookie sheet.

5. Bake in preheated 375°F oven for 15 minutes or until light brown and crusty.

6. Let cool 10 minutes then serve.

Sweet Carrot Halvah

SERVES: 8

INGREDIENTS:

3 cups shredded carrots

½ cup Earth Balance soy butter

2 to 4 tablespoons nondairy cottage cheese

4 cups soy milk

½ cup raisins

½ cup chopped almonds

½ cup finely chopped pistachio nuts

½ cup finely chopped cashews

½ cup finely chopped walnuts

½ cup maple sugar

5 teaspoons ground cardamom

DIRECTIONS:

1. In a large saucepan, sauté the carrots in the butter until they turn red, approximately 5 minutes over high heat.

2. Stir in the cottage cheese and milk. Reduce heat to medium and cook an additional 10 minutes.

3. Add raisins, nuts, maple sugar, and cardamom. Remove from heat.

4. Line a shallow pan with parchment paper or plastic wrap. Put mixture into pan and even out with a rubber spatula.

5. Cover with plastic wrap and let chill overnight in refrigerator.

6. Cut and serve.

Warrior Parfait

MAKES: 1½ pints

INGREDIENTS:

1 scoop protein powder

1 tablespoon chia seeds

1 tablespoon flaxseeds

1 tablespoon coconut flakes

1 tablespoon maca powder

1 tablespoon acai powder

1 tablespoon pomegranate powder

1 tablespoon coca nibs

1 cup blueberries

1½ cups almond milk

½ cup ice

DIRECTIONS:

1. Blend all ingredients in a blender until smooth.

2. Serve immediately.

Groovy Smoothie Fruit Sundae

INGREDIENTS:

Smoothie Topping

1 banana

1 cup strawberries

½ cup blueberries

2 tablespoons walnut butter

1 cup coconut milk

1 cup kale, chopped

½ cup ice

1 tablespoon chia seeds

1 tablespoon flaxseeds

200 mg bilberry extract

Sundae Layers

2 large bananas, sliced

2 cups fresh blueberries

2 tablespoons raw pumpkin seeds

2 tablespoons raw sunflower seeds

2 tablespoons goji berries

2 tablespoons dried cranberries

2 tablespoons gooseberries

DIRECTIONS:

1. Blend all Smoothie Topping ingredients in a blender until smooth.

2. Alternate Sundae Layers ingredients with smoothie toppings in layers.

Tart Cherry and Raspberry Soup

SERVES: 2

INGREDIENTS:

1 cup cherry juice

1 cup unsweetened cherries, pitted

¼ cup dried tart raspberries

1 cup unsweetened coconut milk

3 tablespoons yacon syrup or other sweetener

1 cinnamon stick

DIRECTIONS:

1. In a blender, combine cherry juice, cherries, raspberries, coconut milk, and yacon syrup. Blend until smooth.

2. Pour the mixture into a medium size saucepan, add the cinnamon stick, and bring to a simmer over medium low heat.

3. Cook 10 minutes to enhance cinnamon flavor and longer for a thicker soup.

4. Remove from heat and remove cinnamon stick.

5. Chill 1 to 2 hours.

6. Serve cold.

Raw Chocolate Mint Coconut Cream Cake

SERVES: 2

INGREDIENTS:

Macadamia nut crust

½ cup macadamia nuts

2 teaspoons date paste (see page 213)

½ teaspoon pure vanilla water (see page 213)

A pinch of Himalayan sea salt

¼ cup unsweetened coconut

Almond cream coconut filling

1 cup exotic superfood young thai coconut meat, thawed

2 teaspoons date paste (see page 213)

1 teaspoon pure almond extract

3 tablespoons fresh almond milk (see page 213)

2 tablespoons + 1 teaspoon extra-virgin coconut oil

A pinch of Himalayan salt

Chocolate cream mint filling

1 cup exotic superfood young thai coconut meat, thawed

¼ cup + 3 tablespoons date paste (see page 213)

1½ teaspoons vanilla water (see page 213)

3 tablespoons fresh almond milk (see page 213)

2 tablespoons cacao powder

2 tablespoons + 1 teaspoon extra-virgin coconut oil

A pinch Himalayan sea salt

½ teaspoon pure peppermint flavor

DIRECTIONS:

1. Spray four 4-inch spring form pans with coconut oil.

2. Line all four of the pans with a four-inch round parchment papers.

Continued on page 212.

To prepare the crust:
Using a food processor, fitted with a metal blade, process the nuts until coarsely ground. Pulse in the date paste, vanilla, and salt until well-combined. Add coconut and pulse until well mixed. Remove from processor and firmly press into the two four-inch pans with the parchment paper.

To prepare the almond filling:
Using the food processor fitted with the metal blade, process the coconut meat, date paste, almond extract, almond milk, coconut oil and salt until well combined. Transfer to a Vitamix and blend until smooth for 30 seconds and set aside.

To prepare the chocolate filling:
Using the food processor, fitted with the metal blade, process the coconut meat, date paste, vanilla, almond milk, cacao powder, coconut oil, salt, and peppermint oil until well combined. Transfer to a Vitamix and blend for 30 seconds until smooth.

To assemble the cakes:
1. Divide the chocolate filling into four equal portions. Distribute equally into the four prepared pans and place in the freezer for 15 minutes to set the chocolate.

2. Divide the almond filling into four portions and distribute on top of the chocolate filling. Place in the freezer to set again for 30–40 minutes or until firm.

3. Take a hot knife and run around the inside of pans (with the crust) to loosen the sides. Remove the spring form sides, then take a piece of plastic wrap and place on top of the chilled cake. Turn it over in the palm of your hand and remove the bottom plate of the spring form. Place the crust bottom on a plate.

4. Repeat this process with the remaining pans and stack them on top of crust bottomed plated cakes. Gently compress cake down with a piece of plastic wrap and refrigerate.

Date Paste

MAKES 1 pint
1½ pounds medjool dates, pitted
1 cup water

1. In a food processor fitted with a metal blade, combine the dates and water. Process for 5 minutes until a smooth paste forms.

2. Refrigerate for up to 2 weeks.

Vanilla Water

MAKES 1 pint
2 cups water
7 whole vanilla beans

1. In a blender, combine the water and vanilla beans. Blend for 1 minute on high speed.

2. Store in the refrigerator for up to 1 month.

Fresh Almond Milk

MAKES 1 quart
1½ cups raw almonds soaked in water for at least 6 hours
4 cups water

1. In a blender or Vitamix, combine the almonds and water and blend on high for 5 minutes.

2. Pour into a milk straining bag and squeeze out the milk into a bowl. Discard the pulp.

3. Refrigerate for up to 3–4 days.

Sumptuous Banana Cream Pie

INGREDIENTS:

One prepared crust (see pages 211–212)
6 large sliced bananas
1 cup pure maple syrup
3 tablespoons tapioca flour
1 jar chocolate sauce
2 pints non-dairy ice cream

DIRECTIONS:

1. Evenly distribute the bananas in the prepared pie crust.

2. In a small saucepan combine the maple syrup and tapioca flour. Bring to a simmer and cook over moderate heat for 5 minutes. Pour over the bananas.

3. Drizzle with chocolate sauce and top with non-dairy ice cream.

Almond Butter Frosting

MAKES: 2½ cups

INGREDIENTS:

1 cup almond butter

1 teaspoon almond extract

1 tablespoon carob powder

⅓ cup plus ¼ cup rice milk

¼ cup mashed banana

¼ cup pure maple syrup

1 cup shredded unsweetened coconut

DIRECTIONS:

1. Combine the almond butter, extract, carob powder, milk, banana, and maple syrup in a large bowl.

2. Mix until smooth with an electric mixer.

3. Stir in coconut.

4. Chill at least 30 minutes before using.

Carob Sauce

MAKES: 2 cups

INGREDIENTS:

1²/₃ cups carob chips
½ cup coconut milk

½ cup pure maple syrup
2 teaspoons vanilla extract

DIRECTIONS:

1. Melt the chips in the milk on medium heat.

2. Add the syrup and vanilla and cook until creamy.

3. Remove from the heat, let cool 30 minutes and place on warm cake.

Juices, Shakes, and Smoothies

Amazon Shake

INGREDIENTS:

16 ounces raw almond milk

1 tablespoon maqui powder

1 tablespoon acai powder

2 tablespoons pomegranate powder

2 tablespoons flaxseed oil

1½ bananas

½ cup mixed berries

2 cups ice cubes

DIRECTIONS:

1. Place all ingredients in a blender. Blend until smooth.

2. Serve immediately.

SERVING SUGGESTIONS

- Freeze berries or buy frozen berries and skip the ice.

VERONICA

I ate junk food and was a heavy coffee drinker. I was hypoglycemic and fainted frequently. My skin had ugly eruptions. I cried easily and had low energy. I had several allergies. I lost 15 pounds in this period. Eventually [as I changed my life] all my respiratory infections and skin problems disappeared. I follow the diet and juice during the day, eat fruits in the evening, and make one well planned meal a day. I am now a marathon runner. My energy is without limit. I am healthy.

Sunshine Shaker

MAKES: 1 quart

INGREDIENTS:

1 cup pineapple, chopped

½ cup mango, chopped

1 cup raspberries

1 cup hemp milk

¼ cup pecans

1 banana

1 teaspoon bee pollen

1 scoop protein powder

1 teaspoon camu powder

2 cups ice

DIRECTIONS:

1. Put all ingredients into a blender.

2. Serve immediately.

JOSEPH

I read Gary Null books and listened to *Natural Living* for many years with good results. I have hepatitis, high blood pressure, diabetes, damaged nerves, and recently had a bout of Bell's Palsy. I also have three bulging disks on my spine. With all of these problems, I sought relief and healing.

I decided to follow the protocol. The people that stick to it had good results. Today I juice, no longer use eyeglasses during the day, and am delighted that my blood pressure and diabetes are controlled, and that the Bell's Palsy did not return for two years. I discontinued weight lifting when my back was injured 10 years ago. I recently resumed lifting weights. I have a lot of energy, and the skin on my face is strong. My nails are healthy and pink. As a senior on a fixed income, I cannot afford a nutritionist, however, I study nutrition with Gary's shows and books. Thank you.

Raw Vanilla Coconut Shake

SERVES: 2

INGREDIENTS:

8 ounces raw coconut meat

16 ounces raw coconut water

½ vanilla bean

2 Medjool dates, pitted

1½ cup ice cubes

DIRECTIONS:

1. Blend all ingredients in a blender until smooth.

2. Serve immediately.

GLENROY

I am diabetic and developed cellulitis while serving in the military. I had severe knee and lower back disc pain. I could not climb stairs and used crutches and a cane for two months. Eventually I was paralyzed and confined to a wheelchair. Although my blood pressure and cholesterol were elevated, I ate the typical American diet of flesh foods, wheat, and dairy but beneath it all I desired health.

Since following Gary Null's juicing and detoxification diet, my body went from pain and illness to recovery and joy. My legs are not swollen with cellulites. My backache subsided and circulation is normal. I easily climb three flights of stairs to my apartment. I eat organic foods and use green and red powders and supplements. Life is active. Today I am retired and work with a veteran's council. I love babysitting my granddaughter since I became lighter and energetic. All past symptoms are gone. I am tolerant and learned humility. I focus myself. My body and life are mine.

Mango Berry Smoothie

MAKES: 1 quart

INGREDIENTS:

1 cup mango

1 cup strawberries

1 banana

1 cup nondairy vanilla yogurt

1 tablespoon pumpkin seeds

½ cup ice

500mg ginseng

DIRECTIONS:

1. Blend all ingredients until smooth.

2. Serve immediately.

Breezy Melon Cooler

SERVES: 2

INGREDIENTS:

4 cups watermelon, cubed
1 lime, quartered
1 lemon, quartered
1 green apple, quartered
½ cup mint
1 inch ginger root

DIRECTIONS:

1. Push all ingredients through the juicer.

2. Serve immediately.

228

Brew Away Tension

MAKES: 3 cups

INGREDIENTS:

1 cup broccoli	1 carrot
1 cup cauliflower	3 stalks celery
1 large bunch watercress	1 green apple
1 beet, quartered	1 inch ginger root

DIRECTIONS:

1. Pass all ingredients through a juicer.

2. Serve immediately.

DONNA

Being overweight only became a problem for me in my adult life. In my thirties I went through a difficult divorce. I was emotionally devastated. I had been smoking and drinking to numb the pain. I decided that I would stop smoking and cut back on the wine. But this became more of a hurdle than I had envisioned. I guess I turned to food to fill the void I felt in my gut. I gained weight steadily and kept it on for over ten years. I was unhappy with the way I looked, but I didn't have the will to do anything about it.

I tried a couple of techniques to lose the weight. I tried food combining and met with some success. Shortly after that, I joined the health support group. My general health was not bad, but I was terribly uncomfortable with the extra weight.

I dove right into the protocol. I juice every morning. I have eliminated meat, dairy, and wheat. I take all of the supplements and meditate every morning. I also have read books and listened to several tapes recommended by Gary. The one aspect of the protocol that I have been less than consistent with is exercise. Focusing on being positive, setting boundaries, and detaching from toxic relationships has been very liberating.

I have been in the program for nine months and I have lost about 25 pounds. I am a new, energized person. I have taken control of a situation where I felt dissatisfied and helpless. The protocol has become a way of life.

Fight Back Fusion

MAKES: ½ quart

INGREDIENTS:

½ head of cabbage, chopped

2 carrots

4 celery stalks

4 asparagus stalks

¼ teaspoon cayenne pepper

400mg astragalus

2 tablespoons olive oil

DIRECTIONS:

1. Pass cabbage, carrots, celery, and asparagus through the juicer.

2. Stir in the cayenne pepper, astragalus, and olive oil.

3. Serve immediately.

OLIVER

I weighed 238 pounds. My cholesterol and blood pressure were elevated. I had pain in my chest, pain in my knees and ankles, and frequent heartburn. I was embarrassed by brown age spots on my skin and my eyesight was off. [When I started following Gary's protocol] my weight went from 238 pounds to 188 pounds within 5 months. Blood pressure and cholesterol values were lower. I exercise one to two hours daily, meditate, and use juices and supplements with great enthusiasm. No longer do I have chest pains or heartburn. I feel energetic, less astigmatic, and my hair and nails are healthier. The support group ended but my life just began.

Mellow Yellow Tonic

MAKES: ½ quart

INGREDIENTS:

1 cup papaya

1 cup pineapple, cored and cut into 1-inch cubes

1 lemon, quartered

1 orange, quartered

1 grapefruit, quartered

1 inch ginger root

2 tablespoons aloe vera concentrate

½ teaspoon turmeric

250mg boswellia

DIRECTIONS:

1. Push the papaya, pineapple, lemon, orange, grapefruit, and ginger through a juicer.

2. Stir in the aloe vera, turmeric, and boswellia.

3. Serve immediately.

Rejuvenate and Revive

MAKES: 1 pint

INGREDIENTS:

1 orange, quartered

1 apple, quartered

1 carrot

3 stalks celery

1 inch ginger root

250mg gingko

DIRECTIONS:

1. Push all ingredients through a juicer.

2. Stir in gingko.

3. Serve immediately.

MARIA

I was prescribed Prozac for Multi-Menopausal Syndrome by my gynecologist. I gained weight and lost energy. My hair and nails were weak. I had difficulty sleeping and felt depressed. I thought I followed a sensible eating plan. I did not connect food and aging.

I began the detox protocol carefully and followed it diligently. I wanted to reverse my aging and clean my system out. I lost weight and am keeping it off. I have good energy. My hair and nails are growing to pre-menopausal thickness and strength. I discontinued the Prozac when I began the protocol and am not depressed. I sleep well, look well, and get healthier each day.

Ruby Red Tonic

MAKES: 1 quart + 1 pint

INGREDIENTS:

2 tomatoes, quartered

6 celery stalks

2 cups spinach

2 carrots

1 radish

1 inch ginger root

¼ teaspoon turmeric powder

⅛ teaspoon salt

DIRECTIONS:

1. Pass tomatoes, celery, spinach, carrots, radish, and ginger through the juicer.

2. Stir in turmeric and salt.

3. Serve immediately.

CAROL

Being overweight most of my life caused painful arthritis. My turning point came attending Florida retreats and joining a support group. I quickly adapted to the new lifestyle but hardly exercised. It was when I began yoga lessons that power walking tempted me. It caused joint pain until arthritic symptoms subsided. My energy increased when wheat and dairy were eliminated, and juicing increased. At this point, I became a serious power walker.

I lost 15 pounds the first month on the protocol and felt terrific. Doing support group homework kept me committed to future goals. I moved to a new home, which is uncluttered, and was satisfied to disassociate with the people I felt were obnoxious. I lost 75 pounds. I now belong to a rowing team and race walk with the Gary Null Running and Walking Club.

Electrolyte Energy Spurt

MAKES: 3 cups

INGREDIENTS:

1 cup coconut water

2 tablespoons sunflower seeds

1 apple, quartered

1 peach, seeded and quartered

1 cup cherries, pitted

DIRECTIONS:

1. Pass apple, peach, and cherries through the juicer.

2. Add the coconut water and sunflower seeds to a blender with the juice and blend until smooth.

Clean Green Cooler

MAKES: 20 ounces

INGREDIENTS:

2 cups kale, chopped

2 cups spinach, chopped

1 green apple, quartered

1 cup cucumber, chopped

4 stalks celery

1 inch ginger root

1 lime, quartered

½ cup parsley

200IU vitamin E

200mg COQ10

100mg hawthorne

350mg magnesium

500mg quercetin

DIRECTIONS:

1. Push the kale, spinach, apple, cucumber, celery, ginger, lime, and parsley through the juicer.

2. Stir in the vitamin E, COQ10, hawthorne, magnesium, and quercetin.

3. Serve immediately.

BOB

My life was unmanageable and my stress was overwhelming. I had many allergies and frequent upper respiratory infections. My blood pressure and cholesterol were elevated. I heard about Gary Null's support groups and detoxification. I needed to change and decided to enter a group. That was the beginning of the best part of my life.

How could green juices clean toxins from one's body? Well, that's exactly what happened with good results. My energy built, my head-aches stopped, and cholesterol and blood pressure lowered. I have a new body since exercising, using weights, doing chi gong, and deep breathing. I feel calm, more patient, and less irritable. I love my food and progressive life.

Power Berry Blend

MAKES: 1 quart

INGREDIENTS:

1 cup blackberries
1 cup strawberries
1 cup red grapes
1 cup raspberries
1 red apple, quartered

2 beets, cubed
1 lime, quartered
1000mg vitamin C
500mg quercetin
500mg resveratrol

DIRECTIONS:

1. Push the blackberries, strawberries, red grapes, raspberries, apple, beets, and lime through the juicer.

2. Stir in the vitamin C, querticin, and resveratrol.

3. Serve immediately.

Road Runner

MAKES: 12 ounces

INGREDIENTS:

2 cups pineapple, cubed
1 cup spinach, chopped
1 cup kale, chopped
1 cup grapes

½ teaspoon cayenne pepper
1000mg vitamin C
10mg vitamin B complex

DIRECTIONS:

1. Push the pineapple, spinach, kale, and grapes through the juicer.

2. Stir in the cayenne pepper, vitamin C, and vitamin B.

3. Serve immediately.

LARRY
Carrying around a heavy body caused exhaustion and fatigue. I never exercised and ate the typical American diet. I often had heartburn, probably from sugar in sodas and bad food.

It took some time to get used to drinking juices, but the explanations and respect shown to the people in the group made us enthusiastic. I began to feel the energy growing. I went with it totally: organic, vegan, exercise. I run and power walk. My hair is growing in darker, I lost 20 pounds, and my digestion improved. I still follow the protocol, use the powders and supplements, and love my new body and lifestyle. Thank you Luanne and Gary for helping us understand our lives are in our hands.

Jolly Juice

MAKES: 18 ounces

INGREDIENTS:

3 stalks celery

1 carrot

1 beet, quartered

1 cucumber

1 cup collard greens, chopped

1 cup zucchini, chopped

500mg gotu kola

1 teaspoon manuka honey

DIRECTIONS:

1. Push celery, carrot, beet, cucumber, collard greens, and zucchini through the juicer.

2. Stir in gotu kola and manuka honey.

3. Serve immediately.

NINA

I was diagnosed with lung cancer. I was anemic and had arthritis, almost no energy, and elevated blood pressure. Pain went through me when I walked. I underwent radiation, chemotherapy, and body scans. I was ready for a life change but was not certain where to go or whom to see. After hearing Gary Null on television and radio, I was curious and joined a health support group.

Today I am vegan. I drink green juices and follow the protocol completely. I am cancer-free without medication. My arthritis has diminished, and I can use and enjoy my body by walking, doing yoga, and working in the wardrobe department of a theatrical company. I look forward to a good season with the crew. I am delighted with the results of each new blood test. I have developed personal insight.

Glowing Radiance

MAKES: 1 quart

INGREDIENTS:

1 apple, quartered

4 cucumbers

4 celery stalks

1 lemon, quartered

1 avocado

1000IU vitamin E

1000mg vitamin C

10mg vitamin B complex

DIRECTIONS:

1. Push apple, cucumber, celery, and lemon through a juicer.

2. Blend the avocado, vitamin E, vitamin C, and vitamin B with the juice mixture in a blender.

3. Serve immediately.

Avocados are a power fruit. They are an excellent source of a healthy fat. Like tomatoes, they are an alkaline-forming food that can help balance damaging acids from other foods. Avocados are also a great source of vitamin E. In particular, vitamin E is displayed in avocados in its subtype alpha-tocopherol, the form that is most active in the human body. Thus, eating avocados is one of the most efficient ways to intake Vitamin E which boosts the immune system and can help reduce inflammation.

Orange Grove

MAKES: 1 quart

INGREDIENTS:

2 cups cantaloupe, seeded and cubed

2 cups mango, peeled and cubed

1 grapefruit, quartered

1 orange, quartered

1 lemon, quartered

1 inch ginger root

2 tablespoons aloe vera juice

¼ teaspoon turmeric

DIRECTIONS:

1. Push the cantaloupe, mango, grapefruit, orange, lemon, and ginger root through the juicer. Mix in aloe vera juice and turmeric.

2. Serve immediately.

Perfect Blend

MAKES: ½ quart

INGREDIENTS:

1 beet, chopped

1 cup pineapple, chopped

1 cup grapes

1 cup blueberries

½ banana

1 tablespoon chia seeds

1 tablespoon coconut oil

DIRECTIONS:

1. Push beet, pineapple, and grapes through the juicer.

2. Blend the mixture from the juicer with the blueberries, bananas, chia seeds, and coconut oil.

3. Serve immediately.

Pear Me Up

MAKES: 1 quart + 1 pint

INGREDIENTS:

2 pears, quartered

2 cups pineapple, cubed

1 orange, quartered

1 lemon, quartered

½ cup parsley

1 inch ginger root

30mg zinc

DIRECTIONS:

1. Pass pears, pineapple, orange, lemon, parsley, and ginger root through the juicer.

2. Stir in zinc.

3. Serve immediately.

Pepper Pick Me Upper

MAKES: 2 quarts + 1 cup

INGREDIENTS:

2 yellow peppers, quartered

1 orange pepper, quartered

1 green apple, quartered

4 celery stalks

1 cucumber

1 beet, quartered

1 lime, quartered

1 avocado, peeled

DIRECTIONS:

1. Pass yellow peppers, orange peppers, green apple, celery, cucumber, beets, and lime through a juicer.

2. Add juice and avocado to blender and blend until smooth.

3. Serve immediately.

JAMES

I procrastinated myself into a severe cardiac condition. After my angioplasty, I took blood pressure medication and joined Gary's Walking Club. I was amazed that the walkers and runners, some of whom overcame serious illnesses, were fit and healthy. They made major lifestyle changes. I looked at my life, working 7 a.m. to 9 p.m., without exercise. I was a coffee addict and felt stuck. A change was in order. I joined a group.

If you're going with the protocol, go with it all the way as I did. Organic, juicing, powders, vegan, and life changes. We were a great team, the support group people and me. We are different people today. That's what knowledge does. I am aware of labeling and chemicals. I no longer crave caffeine for energy. I ran in two marathons and confronted my procrastination. I believe in the power of actualization. "Speak the words, live by the words."

Dips and Spreads

Tamari Dip

MAKES: 1 cup

INGREDIENTS:

1 cup nondairy mayonnaise
1 clove garlic, pressed
2 tablespoons tamari

1 tablespoon sesame oil
1 scallion, thinly sliced

DIRECTIONS:

1. Combine all ingredients in a bowl and chill for at least 1 hour before serving.

2. Can be served with the raw vegetables of your choice.

Baba Ghanoush

SERVES: 4-6

INGREDIENTS:

¼ cup red onion, finely chopped, + 1 tablespoon extra virgin olive oil

3¼ pounds eggplant

⅔ cup + 3 tablespoons extra virgin olive oil

1½ teaspoons cumin

¼ cup + 2 tablespoons lemon juice

½ cup + 2 tablespoons sesame tahini

3 cloves garlic

1¼ teaspoons sea salt

¼ teaspoon black pepper

Parsley and cherry tomatoes, to garnish

DIRECTIONS:

1. Sauté the onion in one tablespoon olive oil until caramelized, about 4 minutes. Set aside.

2. Preheat oven 350°F.

3. Pierce eggplants with a fork in several places. Place them in a baking dish and bake in the preheated oven for 40 minutes or until soft to the touch. Set aside to cool.

4. Scrape the eggplant pulp from the skin into a food processor fitted with a metal blade and process for 1 minute. Add olive oil, cumin, lemon juice, tahini, onion, garlic, salt, and pepper. Process an additional 2 minutes.

5. Garnish with parsley and cherry tomatoes.

SERVING SUGGESTIONS

- Serve with fresh greens as a salad.

- Dip with crackers, crudités, or bread.

Pinto Bean Dip

MAKES: 3½ cups

INGREDIENTS:

3 cups cooked pinto beans
½ cup onion, minced
1 clove garlic, minced
1 chili pepper, minced
1 tomato, chopped fine
2 tablespoons tamari
1 teaspoon salt

DIRECTIONS:

1. Mash the beans in a large bowl and add all of the seasonings. If you wish, you may place all ingredients in a blender and puree them.

2. Serve with crackers or use to fill a pita bread and garnish with sprouts for a tasty sandwich.

Avocado Dip

MAKES: 2 cups

INGREDIENTS:

2 avocados

¼ cup scallions, chopped

1 tomato, diced

2 teaspoons nondairy mayonnaise or
    nondairy yogurt

2 tablespoons lemon juice

2 tablespoons pineapple juice

1 sprig of parsley or watercress, chopped
    fine

1 clove garlic

DIRECTIONS:

1. Cut avocados in half. Remove the pit and the meat of the avocado.

2. Put the meat and all other ingredients in a food processor and blend
well.

3. Serve with small pieces of various raw vegetables. It is also delicious
over raw cabbage.

Sweet Onion-Cheddar Delight

MAKES: 1 cup

INGREDIENTS:

½ cup soy cottage cheese

½ cup soy cheddar cheese, grated

1 tablespoon nondairy mayonnaise

¼ cup scallion, sliced

¼ teaspoon black pepper

¼ teaspoon salt

DIRECTIONS:

1. In a food processor, combine soy cottage cheese, grated cheese, mayonnaise, and scallion. Blend well. Mix in pepper and salt.

2. This spread may be served with crackers immediately after preparation. However, the flavor becomes more delightful after the spread has chilled for 1 hour.

Sweet Potato-Broccoli Cream Dip

MAKES: 2½ cups

INGREDIENTS:

1 cup sweet potato, peeled and cubed

½ cup broccoli, chopped

1 cup silken tofu

½ cup tahini

4 tablespoons tamari

1 tablespoon scallions, chopped

¼ teaspoon black pepper, freshly ground

DIRECTIONS:

1. Steam sweet potatoes for 10 minutes.

2. Add broccoli and steam 5 minutes more.

3. In a blender or food processor, combine broccoli, sweet potato, tofu, tahini, tamari, scallions, and pepper until smooth.

4. Serve cold with crackers or pita.

Sweet Potato Hummus

MAKES: 1½ quarts

INGREDIENTS:

2½ pounds sweet potatoes

⅓ cup extra virgin olive oil

2 pounds yellow onions (2 large), diced

2 teaspoons sea salt

½ teaspoon freshly ground black pepper

½ cup tahini (Brad's)

15-ounce can garbanzo beans, rinsed

2 cloves garlic

⅓ cup lemon juice

DIRECTIONS:

1. Preheat oven to 375°F.

2. Bake small sweet potatoes for 45 minutes (if you are using large sweet potatoes increase heat to 450°). Bake until tender, discard skins, and roughly chop.

3. In a skillet over medium low heat, add olive oil, onions, salt, and pepper. Cook until caramelized, about 20 minutes.

4. Add the sweet potatoes, caramelized onions, and the remaining ingredients in a blender or food processor and blend until smooth.

5. Serve at room temperature or chilled with crackers or raw vegetable sticks.

Spicy Tomato Salsa

MAKES: 1½ cups

INGREDIENTS:

1 cup tomatoes, diced

¼ cup red onions, diced

1 tablespoon chopped fresh parsley

3 to 4 tablespoons chopped fresh basil

1 teaspoon salt

½ teaspoon freshly ground black pepper

1 tablespoon extra virgin olive oil

2 tablespoons fresh hot peppers, seeded and minced

DIRECTIONS:

1. Combine all the ingredients in a medium size bowl until well mixed.

2. Chill 1 to 2 hours before serving with chips.

3. It will keep in the refrigerator for 2 days. Stir before serving.

Gourmet Spicy Tofu Dip

MAKES: 1½ quarts

INGREDIENTS:

2 teaspoons apple cider vinegar

1 teaspoon balsamic vinegar

½ teaspoon fresh lemon juice

3 teaspoons dijon mustard

¼ cup fresh basil, chopped

¼ cup fresh parsley, chopped

¼ teaspoon cayenne pepper

3 teaspoons sea salt

¾ teaspoon freshly ground black pepper

2 cups silken tofu

2 avocados, diced

2 cups firm tofu

paprika, garnish

DIRECTIONS:

1. Add to blender apple cider vinegar, balsamic vinegar, lemon juice, mustard, basil, parsley, cayenne pepper, salt, pepper, silken tofu, avocados, and firm tofu.

2. Chill in the refrigerator before serving.

3. Sprinkle with paprika and serve with raw vegetables and crackers.

Protocols

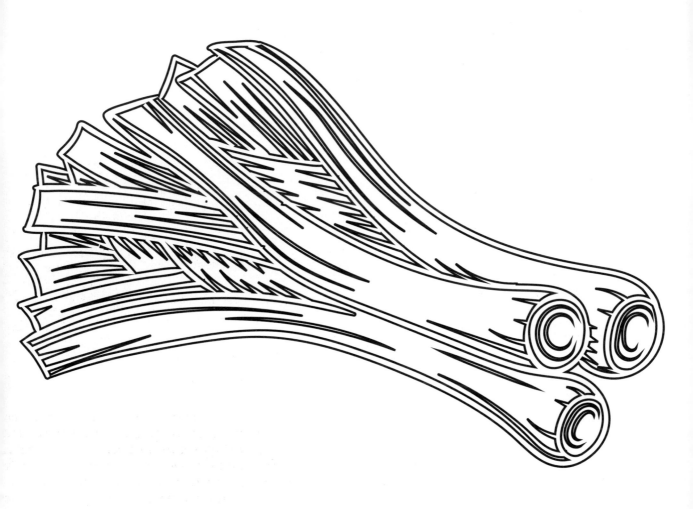

Protocol Disclaimer

The protocols that follow are not in any way to be construed as a prescription to cure a condition, but as nutritional suggestions that are strictly part of an overall healthy lifestyle and behavior modification program.

The protocols must be implemented in gradual steps. Begin with low doses and modest changes. Dietary changes should be introduced gradually so that one undesirable class of food be eliminated each week. For example, it is recommended to eliminate all dairy products the first week, all animal protein the following week, non-organic foods the third week, and so on. It could take up to a year to complete implementing these dietary changes, but it will be easier to maintain.

All of these protocols are meant to be used while following the Living Foods Diet, an organic, plant-based, whole foods regimen rich in vegetables, fruits, fresh juices, whole grains, legumes, seeds, nuts, herbs, and superfoods cooked at low temperatures and free of dairy, animal protein, sugar, refined carbohydrates, foods cooked at high temperatures, processed and denatured foods, preservatives, and additives.

It is always preferable to implement a health protocol under the guidance of a licensed physician.

Suggested dosages listed with the note "as directed" indicates that the supplement should be taken as stated on the bottle or as directed by your healthcare practitioner.

Protocols

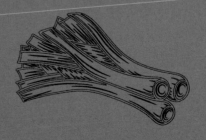

Introduction to Protocols

For the second portion of this book, I will provide protocols for a healthier lifestyle, focusing on positive choices. These protocols will guide you with supplement plans, dietary advice, and other lifestyle choices to help you be your best self. Over time, multiple assaults to the body weaken the immune system through their cumulative effects. For example, various factors that may have weakened the immunity of the baby boomer generation include the following: the above-ground atomic explosions of the 1960s, the massive vaccine programs of the same era, the large consumption of meat that was and still is contaminated with viruses, long-term effects of pesticide toxicity, exposure to lead and mercury, and the widespread use of recreational drugs like marijuana and cocaine. To this list we can add an unhealthy exposure to electromagnetic fields and other sources of low-level radiation at home and at work, as well as exposure to various chemicals on a day-to-day basis. Indeed, thousands of little things that you are not even aware of add up over the years. And then one day you no longer feel fine. Your body has finally passed its threshold barrier and has difficulty repairing itself.

Environmental physician Dr. John Trowbridge of Humble, Texas, explains how this process can produce a "sudden" illness in a seemingly healthy individual:

> One thing doesn't just happen to make your body say, "Wow, that was horrible." Instead, the small daily insults to your body accumulate over time until finally something catastrophic happens. An infection doesn't heal; an unexpected heart attack occurs; joints suddenly hurt and won't stop hurting.

POOR ABSORPTION OF TRACE MINERALS

Even if you receive enough minerals, you may have a difficult time absorbing them. One factor that may affect absorption is the ingestion of antibiotics at high doses and over prolonged periods of time such that the bacterial environment of the colon becomes unbalanced, which lessens its effectiveness in absorbing. Poor absorption can also occur during times of psychosocial stress, when stomach acid and enzymes are not being properly produced. The minerals may be coming in, but they are not properly absorbed because the body is in a hyperactive state that does not allow for the assimilation of food.

IMMUNE HEALTH

Our poor approach to eating in the United States has weakened our immune systems and undermined our health. Sugar, in particular, is weakening our nation because it is being consumed in extreme amounts. Teenagers, for example, may drink an eight-ounce bottle of soda a day, which could contain about seven teaspoons of sugar. Over time, all this sugar can make them more susceptible to infection and to the development of allergies.

Excess sugar in the diet can harm us for a number of reasons. As the body metabolizes ingested sugar, the pancreas produces insulin to remove excess sugar from the circulating blood. The oversecretion of insulin then causes a large drop in blood sugar, or hypoglycemia, and sets the stage for heart disease. For this process, the pancreas requires zinc and manganese. Chromium is utilized to escort the circulating glucose-blood sugar into cells. The B-complex vitamins are also part of this sugar-processing system. These nutrients are thus "used up" as the body struggles with the sugar overload.

Too much sugar can cause blood pressure elevation as well. It decreases our blood circulation by depositing plaque in our blood vessels. Sugar can also decrease function of red blood cells and monocytes (cells that engulf by entering foreign material and consume debris) by entering into them. And it can damage nerve function too.

Even when we attempt to eat well, it's a difficult task because today's foods are not as nutrient dense as those of the past due to poor growing conditions. A store-bought tomato does not feel, look, or taste like one that is homegrown. That could be a sign that it was harvested immature, and lacks minerals and other nutrients. Some studies indicate that consumers now avoid fresh fruits and vegetables because of pesticide contamination. One study conducted at the University of California found that 7 percent of the population had decreased its consumption of fruits and vegetables for this reason.

If you put these two factors together—our poor dietary habits and the lack of nutritious foods—it is easy to see why we run a greater risk of developing health problems as we get older.

Dr. William Rea believes that since our daily diets lack essential nutrients, we need to take supplements such as vitamins A, C, and E, various B vitamins, minerals such as calcium, magnesium, zinc, manganese, and selenium, and some of the amino acids. While these nutrients are indeed necessary for everyone, depending on your personal health, there are even more vitamins and minerals that you should consider adding to your daily regimen (supplementary nutrients are discussed in detail on pages 357–378).

ALLERGIES

Dr. A. Lockyer, who practices internal medicine with a special interest in the role of environmental medicine, toxins, and allergens, believes the term *allergy* is used somewhat loosely these days. The health problems that result from toxic chemical exposures, he says, are actually more of a chemical response than a true allergy. People working in modern unventilated buildings, for example, may become ill from the cumulative effects of concentrated chemicals inhaled that, over time, destroy bodily tissue. This is different from an allergic reaction. "People may get ill from the various chemicals in the carpets," says Dr. Lockyer, "but since the body cannot make antibodies to man-made synthetics, because the body does not recognize these things, it cannot create allergic antibodies to them." The difference between an allergic reaction and a toxic reaction is a matter of dose, since a very minute quantity of pollen or dust may trigger a severe nasal or lung reaction, whereas the level of certain chemicals would have to be many times more concentrated to produce a straight-out poisoning of the body.

However, Dr. John Boyles of Dayton, Ohio, former president of the American Academy of Environmental Medicine, considers sensitivities to chemicals a valid part of allergy medicine. He describes three types of allergies one may develop: to inhalants, to foods, and to chemicals.

As your immune system weakens and your tolerance level lowers, you may become allergic to things that previously didn't bother you. This can create a mushroom effect. First, you are allergic to one thing, and then to two, ten, or even twenty substances. Before, you could tolerate molds, yeast, and fungi. Now you can't. As you become allergic or sensitive to more individual allergens, there is often a progressively greater stress upon your immune-allergy mechanism. When the allergic burden produces a stress on the system, "the straw that breaks the camel's back" leads to other sensitivities, such as arthritis, asthma, and brain allergies (including a number of reactions such as depression, hyperactivity in children, fatigue, headaches, and an inability to think clearly). In extreme cases, allergies are even linked to chronic fatigue syndrome, epilepsy, schizophrenia, autism, and dementia.

Dr. I-Tsu Chao, a doctor of allergy and environmental medicine in Brooklyn, New York, believes we can fight allergies and their negative effects by enhancing the immune system. "The immune system is wonderful, but eating the wrong foods, where the foods can't break down properly, forces the immune system to treat foods like foreign bodies," he says. "This takes away all the immune power and then the viruses can cause trouble. But when we take care of ourselves so that our immune systems don't have to do too much work, we can do very well."

BRAIN HEALTH

Aging successfully in both mind and body requires us to attend to all aspects of our lives: to embrace new challenges, to exercise limbs and cognition, to promote emotional health, and to provide our brains and bodies with the fuel that will allow them to grow healthily from infancy through old age. Research has documented that the brain requires constant stimulation and challenge to develop to its fullest potential. From studies that stress the importance of stimulation in a child's first three years of life, to those that show how using your five physical senses and your emotional sense in unexpected ways will strengthen, preserve, and grow brain cells, science has proven again and again that we must "use it or lose it." Specific training for the brain, such as learning sign language, can boost IQ and promote a lifetime of brain growth—which, if continued, can stave off dementia and other brain diseases as people age. Other brain-challenging activities include taking up a second language, learning to knit, practicing public speaking, or learning to play a musical instrument. The more complex the learning challenge, the more we stimulate our brains and the more vital they remain. Travel, reading, going to museums, and attending book group readings all contribute to an active brain life. The good news is that, young or old, we can continue to learn. So play Scrabble, do crossword puzzles, enjoy bingo, or take up a brand new hobby. Growing older does not mean that we should lose our sense of curiosity in the world around us, or our desire to pursue new challenges.

Most of us know that physical exertion is good for our bodies—but it is also essential for our brains. Exercise should be a natural part of your life, whatever your age. If you do not exercise on a regular basis, or feel that you are too old to embark on a physical fitness program, you can begin to build a stronger body and brain by the simple act of taking a walk. Studies show that senior citizens who walk regularly show significant improvement in memory skills compared to sedentary elderly people. Whether you choose to walk, dance, garden, or practice tai chi or yoga, the most important thing is to get your body moving. The effects of physical activity are beneficial in delaying the onset of dementia and preventing the development of Alzheimer's disease, in addition to improving memory, concentration, and reasoning skills. Exercise also acts as a powerful antidepressant. No matter how old you are, it is never too late to experience the powerful benefits of some kind of physical activity.

Speaking of emotional welfare, as we grow older, we can experience a sense of isolation and perhaps feel like withdrawing from interaction in society. This type of shutting down of emotion, intellect, or spirit is as unhealthy for our brains as the more easily recognized damaging habits of poor diet or lack of exercise. Numerous studies have shown that individuals who have a strong sense of purpose and meaning in their lives thrive in their later years. A positive outlook, and ongoing social and emotional involvement via frequent contact with family and friends, participating in one's community, and feeling satisfied with one's accomplishments are key in maintaining mental health. Practicing meditation may be valuable for brain health as well.

As for nutrition, your brain benefits from: complex carbohydrates (be wary of sugar), fruits and vegetables rich in antioxidants (organic whenever possible; be sure to check out the section on organic produce on pages 333–334), protein, and healthy fats. In the brain health protocol, you'll find the Sixteen Rules of Nutrition that will provide guidance on these food types. Also in this protocol, the suggested supplements have been chosen specifically for their beneficial effects on brain function and health, but you will notice other health benefits as well.

Of course, before you begin any new health program, you should get a comprehensive, full-body evaluation performed by a qualified health care practitioner. A proper health and medical evaluation should evaluate your blood chemistry to assess your blood markers, your metabolic rate, and your blood pressure for indicators of cardiovascular, hormonal, or other imbalances or danger signs. If you are taking medications of any sort, you need to inform your doctor of any supplements you are considering adding to your daily diet, as some may interact with prescription medications.

CANCER

Cancer is a group of diseases in which abnormal cells, instead of being killed by the body's immune system, multiply and spread. The cells no longer follow the rules for the usual orderly progression of growth and become renegades. Cancer can attack any part of the body and may spread to other parts. The sites most often affected are the skin, the digestive organs, the lungs, the prostate gland, and the female breasts. Cancer occurs when cells don't mature, don't repair their mistakes, or don't die. The really tricky part of cancer, the part that can lead to death, is when the aberrant cells migrate. They metastasize and invade other parts of the body, setting up shop in parts distant from their original site. For instance, prostate cancer likes to invade the bones and brain. Breast cancer cells like the bones and the liver. The cancer cells develop the ability to spread by making special enzymes that cut through cell walls and travel through the blood. What makes the cell go haywire? No one can answer for sure. But what can we do to prevent cancer? What can we do to fight cancer once the cells have gone out of control? There is a lot to say in response to these questions. First, poisonous elements from the environment can cause the cell to become cancerous, things like asbestos and cigarettes, so it is important to avoid these things. But it also turns out that some people are more inclined to get cancer than others are. Genetic predisposition and environmental assaults appear to provide the powerful one-two punch.

Among the early warning signs of cancer are a change in bowel or bladder habits; unusual bleeding or discharge; a thickening or lump in the breast, testicles, or elsewhere; an obvious change in a wart or mole; a persistent cough or hoarseness of the voice; a sore throat that does not go away; and difficulty swallowing or indigestion.

In conventional medicine, the usual treatment for cancer is surgery to remove the tumor, radiation to blast away tumors, and/or administration of powerful drugs that find and kill the cancer cells. Unfortunately, these treatments are very difficult to endure and don't always work. Surgery leads to disfigurement. Radiation leads to fibrosis (scarring). Chemotherapy aggressively poisons the body, killing healthy cells along with the cancerous cells, in order to kill the tumor. Chemotherapy drugs are very toxic to healthy cells and can make you feel really sick—your hair falls out, you can't eat, you're weak, and you're deeply fatigued.

Another approach is to try to get the body itself to fight the cancer. Remember that a normal cell has its own maintenance team that repairs damage. If that part of the cell can be bolstered and reactivated, it can do its job of overcoming the tumor-forming oncogenes, reactivating the cell's tumor suppressor genes, and subduing the cancer's growth. Whenever this has occurred, the cancer goes into remission and disappears. Taking care of yourself and living a healthy lifestyle is the best way to start. Engaging in regular physical activity is essential. Volumes of research have established that regular exercise supports the immune system and promotes psychological well-being, which is also critically important. It's been theorized that people who tend to suppress anger are more prone to cancer than others, and that people who are happier and more content with their lives tend to have less cancer and fight it more successfully. It is important to learn to release emotions in a constructive way so as not to be overwhelmed by them. Further, being overweight or obese is especially harmful to the body and the immune system, so it is critical to maintain a normal weight.

Although generally dismissed by the medical establishment as irrelevant, diet and nutritional factors are among the most important contributors to cancer development. Because so many chronic diseases, including cancer, are related to eating a diet poor in phytonutrients, fiber, vitamins, and minerals but rich in fat, processed ingredients, and additives, it is of paramount importance to consider the benefits of adopting a highly nutritious, plant-based diet. Cancer has been linked to diets that are high in fats, animal products—even certain types of vegetable proteins—and processed foods. Pesticides and some types of food additives also can cause cancer. But just as diet can harm you, it can also prevent cancer. Whole-body therapies involve a combination of approaches to cancer treatment and prevention, including diet and nutrition, herbs, immune enhancement, and detoxification. Be sure to carefully review the cancer protocol and comprehensive list of cancer-fighting foods on pages 349–356.

CARDIOVASCULAR DISEASE
There are many causes of heart disease—unhealthy diet, lack of exercise, genetic predisposition, the list goes on and on—but you can do

something about it. You can start by exercising regularly, which improves circulation and gives the heart a healthy workout. (Of course, if an elevated heartbeat or harder breathing is a concern for your condition, you absolutely should talk to your primary care physician before trying a vigorous exercise.) You should also be sure to avoid certain foods like those with excessive sugar, fat, salt, and any processed ingredients. Excess sugar in the diet can harm us for a number of reasons. As the body metabolizes ingested sugar, the pancreas produces insulin to remove excess sugar from the circulating blood. The oversecretion of insulin then causes a large drop in blood sugar, or hypoglycemia, and sets the stage for heart disease. Be aware that calorie-free sweeteners are not a good alternative to sugar. Artificial sweeteners such as aspartame have been shown to contribute to cardiovascular disease as well as weight gain and diabetes. Any foods that unnaturally heighten your blood sugar are to be avoided as much as possible; the long-term effects of chronically high blood sugar include high blood pressure, stroke, heart disease, neuropathies, eye problems, circulatory problems, and kidney disease. Beside sugar, it is recommended that meat should be eliminated from the diet altogether because it is loaded with hormones and chemicals and taxing on the digestive system. A vegetarian diet has been linked to lower risk for metabolic syndrome, hypertension, heart disease, and diabetes.[1] Vegetarians also tend to be thinner than meat eaters and less likely to become inactive.

So what *should* you eat to improve your heart health? Soy improves cardiovascular health in a number of ways. It can lower LDL (bad cholesterol) and raise HDL (good cholesterol), lowering the risk of heart attack and stroke.[2] Studies have also documented flaxseed's favorable effects on

---

1   Glynn, S., "Vegetarians Live Longer Than Meat-Eaters," *Medical News Today*, June 4, 2013, accessed November 25, 2013. www.medicalnewstoday.com/articles/261382.php.

2   Hoie LH, Guldstrand M, Sjoholm A, et al. "Cholesterol-lowering effects of a new isolated soy protein with high levels of nondenatured protein in hypercholesterolemic patients." *Adv Ther*. 2007;24(2):439-47.

heart disease, diabetes, high cholesterol, and osteoporosis.[3,4,5,6] Color can be used as a guide; in general, the stronger and more vibrant the color, the more nutritional value a fruit or vegetable has. It is also important to consume a variety of different-colored foods each day. Different color foods support health in different ways. For instance, whereas green vegetables aid in detoxification, red berries support cardiovascular health. Tomatoes, another red fruit, are high in lycopene, an important nutrient for heart function. Apples contain natural chemicals that provide essential nutrients for improving cardiovascular health by reducing the risk of coronary heart disease and stroke and preventing atherosclerosis. Juicing is an excellent way to get a lot of food-based nutrients in quick, easy servings.

Pay attention to your emotional and psychological health. While the physical heart is an entity all its own, the metaphorical heart plays an important role in our overall wellbeing, too. To this end, you'll find a brief list of suggestions for improving stress management in the protocol for cardiovascular disease. Look through the protocol and discuss the nutrition and supplement guidelines with your physician. If you are taking any medications, you must discuss these and the supplements with your doctor before starting a new regimen as some reactions may occur. Your heart has an important job; taking care of it is a big responsibility, but you can do it if you are ready to be your best self.

3 Mandasescu S, Mocanu V, Dascalita AM, et al. "Flaxseed supplementation in hyperlipidemic patients." *Rev Med Chir Soc Med Nat Iasi.* 2005 Jul;109(3):502-6.

4 Patade A, Devareddy L, Lucas EA, Korlagunta K, Daggy BP, Arjmandi BH. "Flaxseed reduces total and LDL cholesterol concentrations in Native American postmenopausal women." *J Womens Health* (Larchmt). 2008 Apr;17(3):355-66.

5 Inderscience Publishers. "Flaxseed oil may reduce osteoporosis risk." ScienceDaily. www.sciencedaily.com/releases/2009/11/091123114638.htm (accessed February 24, 2014).

6 Dahl WJ, Lockert EA, Cammer AL, Whiting SJ. "Effects of flax fiber on laxation and glycemic response in healthy volunteers." *J Med Food.* 2005;8(4):508-11.

DIABETES

We are repeatedly told there is no cure for diabetes; however, it has been my experience as well as that of many physicians that some patients are able *through a major change in their lifestyle*, including change of diet, to eliminate the symptoms of diabetes. A healthy lifestyle and alternative approaches to treatment in many cases can decrease the amount of insulin or oral medications needed (although type I diabetics will need to continue taking insulin). The natural approach aims to make lifestyle choices, not medication, the center of the program (this does not mean every individual case will see drug use greatly reduced or eliminated). The goal of treatment is to build up the body's ability to function as independently as possible, so that, for example, blood sugar levels are kept low through proper diet. This will not be accomplished overnight. Indeed, part of the natural approach is (generally) to avoid radical changes and opt for gradual transitions. A diabetic who moves from a totally traditional to an alternative approach should never immediately discontinue any diabetic medication. Instead, this patient should work closely with a physician, who would assist in a gradual transition.

Diet, exercise, and a supplement plan are all important aspects of the natural approach to diabetes. Monitoring carbs and protein in the diet are key to turning around your health. A handy formula that many practitioners use as a way to think about the proper relation between food types puts the acceptable ratio of complex carbohydrates to proteins to fats as 50:30:20. While this is a good rule of thumb, a diabetic's personal eating regimen is something that has to be charted by the patient and a nutritionist working together. It should be noted that exercise heightens the body's sensitivity to insulin. The development of type II diabetes often involves poor absorption of insulin by cells whose entrances are clogged. It may be cholesterol that is doing the clogging, and by lowering cholesterol, exercise makes cells more available for glucose assimilation. There is a lot to be studied here, but in short, exercise brings down cholesterol levels, which helps with better insulin usage. In addition to diet and exercise, and detoxification and stress management, I highly recommend a vitamin, mineral, and herbal supplement plan. The protocol in this book is designed to improve blood sugar and take control of the disease.

For type II diabetics, this plan of attack is to be accomplished, in part, through strengthening the thyroid, the secretions of which regulate the overall metabolic rate (the speed of chemical reactions in the body); boosting the adrenal glands that need to work efficiently since they produces cortisone, which can raise or lower blood sugar; and detoxifying the liver, which is often damaged in diabetics. By doing this, the long-term effects of chronically high blood sugar (which include high blood pressure, stroke, heart disease, neuropathies, eye problems, circulatory problems, and kidney disease) can be not only contained but reduced.

MENOPAUSE

The literal definition of *menopause* comes from Greek and means "to pause or cease for a month." It refers to the natural, permanent cessation of a woman's reproductive monthly cycle, or menstruation, and marks the time when a woman's fertility comes to an end. The word is often used interchangeably with the term *perimenopause*, which refers to the years before final menstruation. On average, Western women tend to begin their perimenopausal transition at 47.5 years, with menopause occurring at approximately 51.4 years. As a result of environmental, genetic, and lifestyle factors, the age at the onset of menopause can vary from woman to woman. Recent data indicate that menopausal women are three times more likely to develop Alzheimer's disease and other memory-loss conditions than men are.[7] Postmenopausal women are at a greater risk of low bone density and osteoporosis, which is why half of all women over fifty years old will fracture a bone.

Menopause is a transition that manifests uniquely in each person. Nonetheless, there are a few common symptoms observed among perimenopausal women. These include irregular menstruation, hot flashes, dry skin, mood swings, depression, irritability, vaginal dryness, night sweats, bladder infection, fatigue, and sleep disturbances. Most women will not experience all of these symptoms, and those who do will undoubtedly experience them differently. Evidence that the hormonal changes occur-

---

7 Ibid.

ring at menopause affect mental cognition continues to grow. In fact, foggy thinking and forgetfulness are some of the most common symptoms documented, leading many to postulate that there is more to the menopause-memory link than just age alone. Hormonal changes can also cause weight gain, which is a major factor in cardiovascular disease. Similarly, women at this age have a higher chance of physical inactivity, high blood pressure, diabetes, and high cholesterol.[8] Weight gain and poor dietary habits can increase the likelihood of breast cancer in postmenopausal women. Women need not accept these health problems as a normal part of aging. It is vital that all women follow a healthy lifestyle and focus on prevention as the key tool for combating menopausal risk factors.

Nutrition is an important component of mental function during menopause and andropause. Just as positive dietary choices help maintain good health, poor dietary habits can negatively impact emotions and exacerbate or bring on an episode of depression, which, by extension, can suppress appetite and deter one from getting the proper nutrition so vital to this stage of life. An important benefit of drinking juices daily and eating a well-balanced diet, with an emphasis on organically grown fruits and vegetables, helps to detoxify the body. Furthermore, as you'll find in the menopause protocol, I've developed a core group of vitamins, minerals, and herbs for both men and women. To that, I've added a smaller group of supplements targeted specifically to women and another specifically to men. In addition to these supplement plans, the menopause protocol notes numerous whole-body approaches that can alleviate discomforts and significantly reduce one's risk of degenerative disease.

The remaining three protocols—obesity and weight management, pain, and fatigue—all benefit from a healthy diet in addition to the supplements, therapies, and activities listed in their respective sections. These conditions often intersect with other health problems, and these interrelationships should not be ignored. Rather, they ought to be explored by consulting with

---

8 Angela Salerno, "Hormone Changes during Menopause Increase Risk of Heart Disease and Stroke," *Medical News Today*, February 25, 2010, accessed September 24, 2013, www.medicalnewstoday.com/releases/180249.php.

your doctor, conducting independent research, and perhaps even joining a support group or taking an informational course. As demonstrated by this introduction and the protocols that follow, a healthy diet, supplement plan, exercise, and activities to promote psychological and emotional wellbeing are all critical aspects to a positive lifestyle that can affect real change. If any convincing is still needed, be sure to read the testimonials at the end of each protocol. These success stories come from previous clients and participants in various health seminars and support groups, all focused on natural living and the promotion of wellbeing. My hope is that you will find these guidelines useful starting points as you prepare to start the journey of improvement and a better quality of life. As always, talk to your primary healthcare provider before starting a new supplement plan. Discuss any medications you are taking as some supplements may cause reactions when mixed with certain drugs. Discuss exercises to ensure that you are moving toward a healthier lifestyle in a safe, proactive manner. As a rule, start small, and build your strength and stamina progressively. This is not only a safe approach to starting a new exercise routine but also a more manageable method that will help you to maintain the habit for a long time. In fact, introducing yourself to any positive change in a progressive manner is a good idea—be it dietary changes, adding new supplements, trying a new therapy, or learning a new physical activity. The important thing to remember is this: you are in control of your own health.

Immune Health Protocol

All protocols are to be used only with the professional guidance of a licensed dietician or clinician or physician.

In addition, the protocol does not infer to take all the supplements at one time. Rather it is meant to show all the supplements that have been shown to be beneficial for a condition. Therefore select 2–3 at a time.

Consider the following:

- No smoking or recreational drugs
- Remove mercury fillings

Supplement Suggestions:

Sea vegetable capsules	As directed
Green tea extract	As directed
MGN3 and IP6	As directed
S.O.D.	As directed
Grape seed extract	As directed
Reduced L-glutathione	500 mg
Omega 3 complex	2,000 mg
Vitamin K complex	As directed
Probiotic supplement	As directed
Black cumin seed oil	1 teaspoon 3X/day
DMG	100 mg 3 x/day

High quality multivitamin.. As directed

Kelp.. As directed

L-arginine & L-ornithine.. As directed

White peony extract.. As directed

Astaxanthin.. As directed

Allergies Protocol

All protocols are to be used only with the professional guidance of a licensed dietician or clinician or physician.

In addition, the protocol does not infer to take all the supplements at one time. Rather it is meant to show all the supplements that have been shown to be beneficial for a condition. Therefore select 2–3 at a time.

Most common allergy-related foods in the American diet:

- Yeast
- Milk
- Corn
- Wheat
- Soy
- Egg

Consider:

- Challenging yourself with different foods and eliminating problematic items
- Avoiding processed foods and beverages
- Researching and taking action against environmental stressors
- Homeopathic remedies
- Stress management
- Lessening exposure to electromagnetic radiation
- Exercise
- Magnets
- Alternatives to pesticides
- Safer cleaning products

Suggested Supplements

Beta carotene .... 10,000–20,000 IU/day
Zinc .... 25 mg daily (40–50 mg if you are zinc deficient)
Buffered vitamin C.................... 1,000 mg to begin, slowly increasing
in 500 mg increments
Quercetin..500–1,000 mg daily
GLA.. 500 mg daily
Vitamin E .... 400–800 IU/day from natural mixed tocopherols
Selenium.. 100 mcg daily (200+ mcg daily if
immune system is suppressed)
Vitamin B6 .... 50 mg daily
Vitamin B12.. As directed
Black cumin seed oil .... 1 tsp. 3x daily
Bromelain .... As directed
Butterbur .... As directed
Stinging nettle... As directed
Reishi extract .... As directed

Useful Herbs

Nonspecific Stimulant Herbs

- Echinacea
- Astragalus
- Licorice Root
- Panax
- Siberian Ginseng
- Garlic

Brain Health

All protocols are to be used only with the professional guidance of a licensed dietician or clinician or physician.

In addition, the protocol does not infer to take all the supplements at one time. Rather it is meant to show all the supplements that have been shown to be beneficial for a condition. Therefore select 2–3 at a time.

Sixteen Rules of Nutrition

1. Eat small amounts of nuts and nut butters, such as almond butter and walnuts, as well as sunflower seeds, pumpkin seeds, chia seeds, and sesame seeds.
2. Eat soybeans and soy products.
3. Eat whole grains, such as quinoa, amaranth, spelt, and teff. Include beans (of which there are over seventy varieties commonly available, from black-eyed peas, navy beans, adzuki beans, lentils, split peas, and lima beans, to turtle beans).
4. Eat no dairy, including milk, yogurt, cheese, butter, ice cream, or cream sauces. Replace them with rice milk, soy milk, almond milk, or oat milk. Do not use any nondairy product with casein in the ingredients.
5. Eat no animal meat, fish, or shellfish.
6. Use no caffeine or alcohol. This means cutting out chocolate, coffee, tea, wines, hard liquor, and beer. Replace them with decaffeinated herbal teas and grain beverages, such as Postum, Cafix, Raja's Cup, or green tea (which has small amounts of caffeine but also has threonine, which neutralizes caffeine and has a very beneficial calming effect).

7. Eat no processed sugar or artificial sweeteners. If you must use a sweetener beyond what naturally occurs in food, choose stevia root, raw unfiltered honey, molasses, brown rice syrup, or natural food sweeteners. You can also use chromium picolinate 200 mcg to curb sugar cravings.

8. Drink no carbonated beverages, including sodas or seltzer. Replace them with spring water, distilled water, filtered water, or fresh-squeezed organic juices.

9. Eat no processed bread or wheat products. Replace them with spelt bread, sprouted whole-grain bread, rice bread, or Essene bread. Make sure to read the labels to ensure that these products do not have refined flours, sugars, or trans fats.

10. Eat only certified organic produce. This applies to all vegetables, fruits, beans, grains, legumes, nuts, seeds, and potatoes.

11. Eat no deep-fried or processed foods. Replace them with steam-fried, sautéed, steamed, stir-fried, or broiled meals.

12. Try to avoid using oils for cooking, or keep the amount extremely low. Every tablespoon of oil costs you 120 calories, and all oils damage the endothelium, the delicate lining of the arteries. If you must use oil, choose healthier oils for cooking, such as macadamia and safflower oils. For baking, use hazelnut, macadamia, coconut, or mustard seed oils. For salads, use walnut, flaxseed, or extra virgin, cold-pressed olive oil.

13. Eat no food additives, preservatives, coloring agents, flavorings, or MSG.

14. Eat no bedtime snacks. Eat primarily during the day. Try to have your largest meal between 1:00 and 3:00 p.m., with a light breakfast, and a very light dinner.

15. Avoid dehydration. Make sure you drink plenty of fluids throughout the day. It's important not to lose our liquid balance, because we will then upset our electrolyte balance, our lymphatic balance, and our cleansing and elimination program. Most people should have a minimum of one gallon of water per day, but if you are sweating profusely or exercising vigorously, more might be needed. It is best to have an impedance test, which will determine what percent of your body is water. Ideally it should be between 72 and 74 percent, because for each percentage under that, you will be losing your body energy and lessening the process of cleansing and detoxification. Liquids can include purified water or juices, plus one or two cups of green tea daily, lemon juice to help alkalize the body, and digestive enzymes to help with the tea.

16. Make no excuses. Keep a positive outlook and be sure to appreciate how your body and brain begin to feel and act younger after just a short time following this protocol. Commit to healthy living habits and maintain them for the sake of your long-term mental and physical health.

Suggested Supplements

Acetyl-L-carnitine.............................. 2,000 mg in two divided doses
Alpha-lipoic Acid................................ 300 mg in two divided doses
B-complex Vitamins
    B1 ....75 mg thiamine
    B2 ....50 mg riboflavin
    B3 .... 200 mg niacin
    B5 .... 500 mg pantothenic acid

B6 .... 75 mg pyridoxine
B8 .... 250 mg inositol
B9 .... 800 mcg folic acid methylated
B12 .... 800 mcg methylated
Biotin .... 60 mcg
Trimethylglycine (TMG) .... 200–300 mg
Choline .... 250 mg
Para-aminobenzoic acid .... 100 mg
Carnosine .... 1000 mg
Coenzyme Q10 (coQ10) .... 100–300 mg
Dehydroepiandrosterone (DHEA) .... 25–50 mg (should not be
taken by individuals with
hormone-related cancers)
Dimethylaminoethanol (DMAE) .... 150 mg (may be overstim-
ulating for some people;
consult your doctor)

Omega 3 Complex.. As directed
Glycerylphosphorylcholine (GPC) .... 600 mg
Lecithin .... 1 g
Phosphatidylcholine... 500–1,000 mg
Phosphatidylserine (PS).................... 300 mg (do not use if you have
bipolar disorder are suffer
from depression)
Pregnenolone .... 20 mg (should not be taken by individuals
with hormone-related cancers)
Proanthocyanidins .... 200 mg (naturally occur in grape seed
extract and pine bark extract)
Selenium.. 200 mcg
Resveratrol .... 200 mg

Ginkgo Biloba .... 200 mg

Panax Ginseng .... 200 mg

Choline... 500 mg

Inositol .... 500 mg

Vinpocetine ....10 mg 2X day with meals

Vitamin C ....up to bowel tolerance 6X/day

Vitamin E .... 400–800 IU/day from natural mixed tocopherols

Wild blueberry extract .... As directed

Grape seed extract .... As directed

Gastrodin... As directed

Ashwagandha .... As directed

Black cumin seed oil .... 1 tsp. 3x daily

Resveratrol ....250 mg daily

Vitamin K2 .... As directed

Alpha-glycerylphosphorylcholine (GPC) .... 600 mg

Cancer Protocol

All protocols are to be used only with the professional guidance of a licensed dietician or clinician or physician.

In addition, the protocol does not infer to take all the supplements at one time. Rather it is meant to show all the supplements that have been shown to be beneficial for a condition. Therefore select 2–3 at a time.

Consider the following:

- Diet
- Antioxidant supplements
- Herbs
- Exercise
- Beneficial practices for mental welfare

Suggested Antioxidant Supplements (daily doses):

Vitamin C .... up to 12g, divided throughout the day (50–100 g if intravenous)

Alpha-Lipoic acid .... 250–500 mg

Omega 3 complex .... containing 1,000 mg of perilla oil; 1,000 mg of flaxseed oil

Vitamin A .... 4,000–7,000 IU (less if beta-carotene is taken)

Beta-Carotene ....20,000–30,000 IU

Carotenoids .... 9–20 mg of sulforaphane; 10–30 mg of lycopene; 15–40 mg of lutein

Vitamin E .... 400–800 IU with natural mixed tocopherols

Vitamin K .... 2 mg

Selenium .... 200 mcg

Silibinin (Milk Thistle) .... 100 mg 2X/day

L-glutathione .... 500 mg

Superoxide dismutase and catalase .... 100 IU

Coenzyme Q10 .... 500 mg

Grape seed extract .... As directed

Glutamine .... 2 g or more (not to exceed 14 g daily)

Black cumin seed oil .... 1 teaspoon 3X/day

Curcumin .... As directed

Green tea extract .... As directed

Pomegranate extract .... As directed

Additional Supplements (daily doses)

Dehydroepiandrosterone (DHEA) .... 25 mg

Melatonin .... 2 mg

Digestive enzymes .... As directed

Conjugated linoleic acid (CLA) .... 1,000 mg 6X/day for
cancer patients

Modified citrus pectin .... 6–10 g

Lactoferrin .... 300–900 mg

N acetyl cysteine .... 2,000 mg

Olive leaf extract .... As directed

Resveratrol .... 200–300 mg

Zinc .... 25 mg

Chromium .... 200 mcg

Genistein .... As directed

Vitamin D3 .... 5,000–7,000 units daily
High quality mushroom complex .... As directed
Cat's claw .... As directed
Bilberry extract .... As directed
Modified citrus pectin .... As directed

Dietary Suggestions

- Incorporate 2–3 servings of cruciferous vegetables such as kale, cauliflower, Brussels sprouts, broccoli, and cabbage into your daily diet.
- Eat 4 oz. of broccoli sprouts daily.
- Drink 8 oz. of unsweetened pomegranate for heart disease 2X daily.
- Drink 2 oz. of wheat grass juice, 1 oz. lemon juice, 2 oz. ginger juice, 2 oz. aloe vera juice diluted with green apple, cucumber, or celery juice 2X daily.
- Drink one 16 oz. cabbage juice daily.
- Consume 1 tablespoon of olive oil 2X daily.

Useful Herbs

- Aloe Vera
- Astragalus
- Ginkgo Biloba
- Echinacea
- Garlic
- Ginger
- Turmeric
- Ginseng

- Theanine
- Lentinan
- Red Clover
- Essiac
- Hoxsey Herbal Therpay
- Berberine-Containing Herbs
- Feverfew

Anticancer Foods:

- Alkaline Foods
- Fruits & Berries
- Vegetables
- Whole Grains
- Beans/Legumes
- Seeds
- Cruciferous Vegetables
- Green Foods
- Red Foods
- Fiber
- Fresh-Squeezed Juices
- Green Tea
- Mushrooms
- Macrobiotic Foods
- Seaweeds
- Spices

Things to Avoid:

- Meat
- Dairy Products
- Antibiotics
- Pesticides
- Tobacco
- Alcohol
- Radiation
- Electromagnetic Radiation (EMR)
- Processed Foods

Beneficial practices for mental welfare:

- Hypnosis
- Breathing exercises
- Massage
- Aromatherapy
- Yoga
- Positive visualization

Whole body approaches:

- Gerson Therapy
- Issels Treatment (formerly *Ganzheit* Therapy)
- Eclectic Triphasic Medical System (ETMS)
- Antineoplaston Therapy
- Dr. Nicholas Gonzalez's Enzyme Therapy

Cardiovascular Disease Protocol

All protocols are to be used only with the professional guidance of a licensed dietician or clinician or physician.

In addition, the protocol does not infer to take all the supplements at one time. Rather it is meant to show all the supplements that have been shown to be beneficial for a condition. Therefore select 2–3 at a time.

Dietary Suggestions

Fiber (daily total) .... 50 g
Pectin .... 5 g
Fat calories .... 20% of all calories

Supplement Suggestions

Folic acid .... 2 mg methylated
Niacin .... 110 mg
B-6 .... 150 mg
Vitamin C .... up to bowel tolerance 6 x/day
Vitamin E .... 400–800 IU/day from natural mixed tocopherols
Chromium .... 200 mcg
Calcium (citrate) ...1200 mg in the morning and 400 mg at nighttime
Magnesium (citrate) .... 900 mg
Selenium .... 200 mcg

L-arginine .... 500 mg
Vitamin D3 ....2,000 units
Betaine .... As directed
L-Carnitine ....1,000 mg
Bioflavanoids .... As directed
Coenzyme A .... As directed
Coenzyme Q10 ....200 mg 3 X/day
Glycosaminoglycans... 200 mg
Lecithin .... As directed
Omega 3 fatty acids ....3,000 mg
L-taurine .... 500 mg
Garlic ....4,000 mg
Citrin .... 50 mg
Reduced L-glutathione .... 500 mg
NAC ....1,500 mg
Policosinol .... 10 mg
DHEA... 25 mg
B complex... 50 mg
Melatonin .... 1 mg
Potassium .... 500 mg
DMG (sublingual) .... 150 mg 4 x/day
TMG.. 200 mg 3 x/day
Phosphatidyl choline................................... 500 mg 2 x/day
Flaxseed oil...2,000 mg
Quercitin ....2,000 mg
NADH .... 20 mg 4 x/day
Hawthorn .... As directed
Evening Primrose Oil... 200 mg
Ginkgo biloba .... 200 mg
Astaxanthin.. As directed

Resveratrol .... As directed
Arjuna extract .... As directed
PQQ .... As directed
Olive leaf extract.. As directed
Celery seed extract.. As directed
Cayenne pepper capsules .... As directed
Black cumin seed oil .... 1 teaspoon 3X/day

Other considerations:

- Oriental Bodywork (acupuncture, AMMA™ therapy)
- Stress management
- Neurolinguistic Therapy
- Meditation 30 minutes a day
- Individualized exercise program

Add the following to your juicing regimen for high blood pressure:

- Wasabi
- Radish
- Garlic
- Ginger

Suggested Supplements for Coronary Heart Failure

Take as directed:
Feverfew: anti-thrombotic
Garlic: increases clotting time
Gingko: cardio protective, increases contractile functioning
Red Ginseng: synergistic with Digoxin; improves hemodynamics

Green tea extract: decreases platelet aggregation

Phosphatidyl serine: anti-coagulant

Thiamine (Vitamin B1): synergistic with Lasix; cardioprotective

Vitamin C: decreases platelet aggregation

Vitamin E: decreases platelet aggregation

L-Carnitine: increases oxygen uptake by cells

Nattokinase: thrombolytic enzyme

Vinpocetine: for overall circulation, decreases blood pressure and prevents platelet aggregation

Suggested Supplements for high cholesterol:

Comprehensive fiber formula... As directed
Apple pectin .... As directed
Policosanol.. As directed
Garlic .... 8,000 mg/day
Cayenne (not if taking cardiac meds)............................ As directed
Curcumin .... As directed
Gugulipid .... As directed
ECGC .... As directed
Ginger .... As directed
Omega complex ....1,500 mg 2 x/day
Vitamin B6 .... As directed
Lecithin .... As directed
Vitamin C .... Up to bowel tolerance 6 X/day
Niacin (Vitamin B3) ....150–500 mg/day
Vitamin E .... 400–800 IU/day from natural mixed tocopherols
Selenium... 200 mcg/day
Perilla Oil (EFA) .... As directed

Diabetes

All protocols are to be used only with the professional guidance of a licensed dietician or clinician or physician.

In addition, the protocol does not infer to take all the supplements at one time. Rather it is meant to show all the supplements that have been shown to be beneficial for a condition. Therefore select 2–3 at a time.

Consider the following:

- Exercise
- Avoiding processed foods
- Stress management
- Challenging yourself with different foods and eliminating problematic items

Super Foods to Combat Diabetes:

- Apples
- Apricots
- Bananas
- Blueberries
- Broccoli
- Carrots
- Garlic
- Ginger
- Goji Berries
- Green Teas
- Legumes

- Leafy Vegetables
- Mushrooms
- Onions
- Oranges
- Peppers (capsicum)
- Soy
- Tomatoes
- Whole Grains

Suggested Supplements

Chromium Picolinate ....200 mcg
Vitamin C ....up to bowel tolerance 5X/day
Biotin..500 mcg
Vitamin B6 .... 100 mg
Vitamin B12...1 mg methylated
Vitamin E ....400–800 IU natural mixed tocopherols
Calcium Citrate...1,000 mg
Magnesium Citrate...1,000 mg
Potassium .... 200 mg
Manganese... 15 mg
Zinc .... 30 mg
Selenium...200 mcg
Quercetin...1,000 mg 2×/day
EFAs (Essential Fatty Acids) .... 3,000 mg/day
GLA... 500 mg 2×/day
L-Carnitine .... 500 mg 2×/day
Inositol .... 500 mg
L-Glutamine .... As directed
Vanadyl sulfate .... As directed

Garlic ....1,000 mg 2×/day

Bitter melon... 100 mg

Gymnema syvestre .... As directed

Ginseng .... 100 mg

Aloe vera .... 3 tsp/day

Alpha Lipoic acid .... 600 mg

Grape seed extract .... 200 mg 3×/day

NAC .... 500 mg 2×/day

Coenzyme Q10 ....200 mg 2X/day

Curcumin .... As directed

Dandelion extract... As directed

Evening primrose oil ....1,000 mg

Sea vegetable powder.. As directed

Maitake complex.. As directed

Proteolytic enzymes... As directed

Fiber complex[a] .... As directed

R-lipoic acid...210–420 mg daily

Carnosine .... 500 mg 2×/day

DHEA[b]... 25 mg early in the day

EPA/DHA................................. 1,400 mg EPA and 1000 mg DHA

Silymarin[c] .... As directed

Green tea extract ....725 mg green tea extract (minimum 93% polyphenols)

Ginkgo biloba .... 120 mg daily

Bilberry Extract .... 100 mg daily

Cinnamon extract[d] .... As directed

Coffee berry extract[e].. As directed

R-Lipoic acid... As directed

Sorghum bran extract.. As directed

Mulberry leaf extract .... As directed

Phloridzin.. As directed

Benfotiamine .... As directed

Ashwagandha .... As directed

Black cumin seed oil .... 1 teaspoon 3X/day

[a]Your diet should have 30–50 grams of fiber a day; if not, have 15 grams with a beverage at night.

[b]After 3–6 weeks of taking DHEA, follow up with blood testing to ensure optimal levels.

[c]This silymarin should contain 900 mg silybum marianum standardized to 80% silymarin, 30% silibinin, and 4.5% isosilybin b.

[d]Cinnamomum cassia standardized to .95% trimeric and tetrameric a-type polymers (1.2mg).

[e]Coffee Arabica extract (whole fruit) standardized to 50% total phenolic acids (5o mg) and 15,000 micromoles per gram oraC.

Dietary Recommendations for Diabetics

· Chlorophyll drinks throughout the day

· Complex carbohydrates, such as lentils, peas, steel-cut oatmeal, whole grain pasta, and brown rice

· Raw and cooked vegetables. Carrots, beets, and corn are high glycemic foods; keep them to a minimum. Watermelon, blueberries, and apples have a lower glycemic index.

· Consume 3–4 servings of protein/day (soy, grains and beans, quinoa, protein shake).

· Bean pod tea, which tonifies the kidneys and adrenal glands.

· It is recommended to graze, or eat small quality meals throughout the day. Examples of these meals include an avocado or hummus salad, bean soup, raw nut and pomegranate salad, or a tempeh and wild mushroom sauté.

Herbs and Plants for Diabetes and Insulin Production:

- Cichorium intybus (chicory)
- Rauwolfaia serpentine (Indian snakeroot)
- Thymus vulgaris (common thyme)
- Arctium lappa (gobo)
- Carthamus tinctorius (safflower)
- Passiflora edulis (maracuya)
- Opuntia ficus-indica (Indian fig)
- Taraxacum officianale (dandelion)
- Tetrapanax papyriferus (rice paper plant)
- Canavalia ensiformis (jack bean)
- Linum usitatissimum (flax)
- Pueraria lobata (kudzu)
- Hordeum vulgare (barley)
- Inula helenium (elecampane)
- Althea officinalis (marshmallow)
- Oenothera biennis (evening primrose)
- Avena sativa (oats)
- Triticum aestivum (wheat)
- Medicago sativa (alfalfa)
- Panicum maximum (guinea grass)
- Cocos nucifera (coconut)
- Plantage major (common plantain)
- Dandelion root
- Blueberry
- Ginkgo biloba
- Banaba and ampalaya Cedar Berry Cranberry
- Ginger Burdock Alfalfa Goldenseal Ginger
- Pau D'Arco Juniper Berries Fenugreek
- False Unicorn Root
- Onion

Menopause

All protocols are to be used only with the professional guidance of a licensed dietician or clinician or physician.

In addition, the protocol does not infer to take all the supplements at one time. Rather it is meant to show all the supplements that have been shown to be beneficial for a condition. Therefore select 2–3 at a time.

Avoid these inflammatory aggravators:

- Meats
- Sugar
- Caffeine
- Alcohol
- Tobacco
- Pesticides

Consider the following:

- Eliminate meat, including beef and poultry, shellfish, swordfish, catfish, and shark.
- Eliminate dairy, including milk, yogurt, cheese, butter, ice cream, cream sauces, and anything containing casein. Replace with non dairy milks (rice, soy, nut, and silken tofu).
- Eliminate non-organic produce. Replace with organically grown fruits, vegetables, grains, and beans. We recommended nine servings of fruits and vegetables a day, and four servings of beans/legumes and grains.

- Eliminate wheat. Replace with spelt bread, sprouted whole-grain bread, rice bread, millet bread, and Essene bread, as well as pastas, pancakes, and waffles made from spelt, buckwheat, quinoa, and rice.
- Eliminate sugar and artificial sweeteners. Replace with stevia, agave nectar, organic kiwi sugar, raw honey, molasses, barley malt, and brown rice syrup. (Chromium picolinate, 200 mcg, was recommended to relieve sugar cravings.)
- Eliminate caffeine and alcohol, including chocolate, coffee, tea, colas, wines, hard liquor, and so forth. Replace with herbal teas, Mu tea, twig tea, grain beverages (e.g., Cafix), decaffeinated green tea and decaffeinated white tea (not black or oolong tea).
- Eliminate carbonated drinks, including soda and seltzer. Replace with spring, distilled, or filtered water; lemon water; fresh-squeezed organic fruit juice; iced herbal tea, Teeccino, or soy coffee; and coconut juice or water.
- Eliminate fried and processed foods. Replace with steamed, sautéed, stir-fried, grilled, or broiled foods.
- Eliminate chemicals, including food additives, preservatives, coloring agents, and artificial flavorings. Avoid MSG. Use non-irradiated spices and flavorings, such as Herbamare, sea salt, granulated dulse, and other sea vegetables; sesame seeds; organic, wheat-free soy sauces; and salad dressings consisting of olive oil, lemons, spices, and balsamic vinegar.
- *Include* the following beneficial foods in the diet as well: sprouts, sea vegetables, onions, garlic, and healthy oils. For cooking, use coconut, macadamia, and mustard seed oils. For baking, use hazelnut and macadamia oils. For salads and to add to cooked foods, use flaxseed oil; extra-virgin, cold-pressed olive oil; safflower oil; seed oils (grape, sesame, sunflower); avocado; and nut oils (almond, walnut, hazelnut, peanut).

- Take 1 teaspoon of coconut oil, flaxseed oil, and black cumin seed oil daily.
- Take a probiotic supplement supplying 5–10 billion CFU daily.
- Drink fresh juices. Participants started with one glass of green juice per day and built up to eight glasses per day in week twelve. The juice consisted of four ounces of dark and light green vegetables and six ounces of fluid, or one tablespoon of chlorophyll-rich green powder and ten ounces of fluid (e.g., milk substitute, cooled herb tea, diluted vitamin water, organic fruit juice, or filtered water). To this, one ounce of aloe concentrate and one teaspoon of red fruit powder were added.
- You can even make a gallon of fresh green juice to be used over a week. Ingredients include one to two bunches of organic celery, one to two bunches of organic parsley, four to five organic cucumbers, four organic lemons or limes, four to five organic apples, and optional foods such as cruciferous vegetables (purple cabbage, cauliflower, broccoli), green leafy vegetables (kale, chard, collards, mustard greens, arugula, spinach, bok choy), ginger, dill weed, fennel, scallions, onions, garlic, mint, cilantro, and other natural spices and flavorings. Carrots, tomatoes, or beets could be added for sweetness, but only in limited amounts for people with imbalances related to sugar consumption.
- Engage in aerobic exercise for 60 minutes 5X/week.

Supplements for Both Men and Women

Vitamin A ....10,000 IU
Vitamin B1 (Thiamine Mononitrate) .... 25 mg
Vitamin B2 .... 50 mg

Vitamin B6 .... 50 mg
Vitamin B12 (Cyanocobalamin) .... 1 mg methylated
Folic Acid.. 1 mg methylated
Vitamin C (in divided doses) .... 5,000 mg
Vitamin E .... 400–800 IU/day from natural mixed tocopherols
Vitamin D3 .... 3,000 IU
Pantothenic Acid (D-Calcium Pantothenate) .... 300 mg
Choline Bitartrate .... 150 mg
Inositol .... 150 mg
Calcium Citrate .... 1,000 mg
Magnesium Citrate .... 1,000 mg
Zinc .... 15 mg
Selenium .... 100 mcg
Copper .... 2 mg
L-Carnitine .... 1,000 mg
Acetyl-L-Carnitine Arginate HCL .... 500 mg
L-Carnosine (in Divided Doses) .... 2000 mg
L-Cysteine .... 200 mg
L-Glutamine .... 500 mg
L-Taurine .... 100 mg
L-Tyrosine .... 100 mg
N-Acetyl Cysteine .... 800 mg
Alpha Lipoic Acid .... 500 mg
Resveratrol .... 200 mg
Grape seed extract .... 200 mg
Coenzyme Q10 .... 100 mg 4X/day
Glucerophosphorylcholine .... 250 mg
Quercetin .... 1,000 mg
Phosphatidyl-Serine .... 200 mg

Pycnogenol .... 100 mg
DHEA (if blood chemistry or saliva level shows deficiency) ... 15 mg
Astaxanthin .... 25 mg
Benfotiamine .... 50 mg
Bromelain .... 100 mg
Lutein .... 25 mg
Lycopene .... 25 mg
Rutin .... 100 mg
Bilberry Fruit Extract .... 25 mg
Blue Cohosh .... 100 mg
Broccoli Stem .... 25 mg
Cabbage Leaf .... 25 mg
Carrot Root .... 25 mg
Cayenne .... 50 mg
China Green Tea Leaf Powder .... 200 mg
Citrus Bioflavonoid .... 300 mg
Ginkgo Biloba Leaf .... 100 mg
Licorice Root .... 25 mg
Milk Thistle Leaf .... 25 mg
Raspberry Leaf Powder .... 5 mg
Rosemary Leaf Powder .... 25 mg
Siberian Ginseng Root .... 100 mg
Ginkgo Biloba .... 200 mg

Additional Supplements for Women Only:

Chasteberry fruit powder .... As directed
Dong quai root .... As directed
EPA/DHA .... 1,400/1,000 mg

Flaxseed oil .... 1–3 tbsp.
GLA .... 285–1,400 mg
L-theanine .... 100–200 mg
5HTP .... As directed
Pomegranate extract .... 200 mg
Red clover blossom extract .... As directed
Soy bean extract .... 500 mg
St. John's wort .... As directed
Vitex berry extract .... As directed

Additional Supplements for Men Only:

Cernitin .... 100 mg
Chrysin (do not take if you have prostate cancer) .... 1,500 mg
Citrus pectin .... 220 mg
Milk thistle seed .... As directed
Muira puama .... As directed
Phytosterol complex .... As directed
Piperine .... 10 mg
Pygeum bark extract .... As directed
Saw palmetto berry extract .... As directed
Soy germ powder .... 120 mg
Stinging nettles .... As directed

Obesity and Weight Management Protocol

All protocols are to be used only with the professional guidance of a licensed dietician or clinician or physician.

In addition, the protocol does not infer to take all the supplements at one time. Rather it is meant to show all the supplements that have been shown to be beneficial for a condition. Therefore select 2–3 at a time.

There are usually specific issues around weight gains:

- Thyroid imbalance, which often points to a toxic liver.
- Overeating due to eating on the run, social/cultural expectations.
- Blood sugar imbalance leads to cravings.
- Poor circulation, low energy from a sedentary lifestyle.
- Poor elimination.
- Menopause.
- Genetic predisposition.

Consider the following protocol for weight management:

- Four 10 oz glasses of green juice each day: 1 tbsp green powder + 10 oz water or 4 oz fresh juiced dark and light green vegetables + 6 oz water.
- Any high quality multivitamin that includes pantothenic acid 500 mg, chromium picolinate 100 mcg, magnesium, and alpha lipoic acid.

- Two meal replacement protein shakes daily containing at least 20 g of plant-based protein (may mix with vegetable juices).
- Consuming several small meals throughout the day (grazing).
- Two protein shakes daily with 20 g protein per shake.
- Work up to power walking, swimming, or other aerobic exercise for 45 minutes daily, three times per week.
- Fast one day a week with a healthy liquid diet of juices.

Supplement suggestions:

Omega 3 Complex...3,000 mg
Vitamin D3 ....2,000 units
Grape seed extract .... As directed
CLA..3,000 mg
Coenzyme Q10 ....100 mg 3X/day
Vanadyl sulfate .... As directed
Lecithin or niacinamide .... As directed
Inositol .... As directed
L-carnitine ....500 mg 2X/day
L-methionine .... 400–800 mg
Calcium/magnesium (citrate)... 900 mg
DHEA... 25 mg
GABA .... As directed

After eight weeks add:

Sea vegetable supplement .... As directed
L-Taurine .... As directed

L-glutamine ....2,000 mg at night

Iodine (potassium iodide) .... As directed

Vitamin B12... 1 mg methylated

Melatonin .... 1 mg at night

L-Tyrosine.. As directed

B-Complex .... As directed

White mulberry leaf extract .... As directed

Green tea extract .... As directed

Diuretic quality foods:

- Celery, cucumber
- Watermelon
- Dandelion
- Asparagus
- Parsley

Other aids:

- Amla, an ayurvedic herb that reduces body fat
- Borage seed, hawthorn berry, licorice root help adrenals and thyroid
- Green tea, cinnamon, and cayenne aid in weight loss
- Guggul, an ayurvedic remedy, normalizes cholesterol and tri-glycerides
- Triphala, an ayurvedic herb that rejuvenates glandular function

Pain Protocol

All protocols are to be used only with the professional guidance of a licensed dietician or clinician or physician.

In addition, the protocol does not infer to take all the supplements at one time. Rather it is meant to show all the supplements that have been shown to be beneficial for a condition. Therefore select 2–3 at a time.

Suggested Supplements

Niacin.. 500 mg
Feverfew capsules... As directed
Coenzyme Q10 .... 300 mg
Vitamin B12...1 mg methylated
Magnesium Citrate.. 500 mg
Calcium Citrate... 500 mg
Quercetin ....1,000 mg
Bromelain .... As directed
Glutamine.. 2,000 mg/day
Melatonin .... 1 mg
Omega 3 complex .... As directed
L-Arginine .... As directed
Ginger .... As directed
Gingko Biloba .... As directed
Valerian .... As directed
5HTP .... As directed
Royal jelly for B vitamins .... As directed

Evening Primrose oil .... As directed
Butterbur Root for preventive care .... As directed
Black cumin seed oil .... As directed
Curcumin .... As directed
Boswellia serrata extract .... As directed
Tart cherry extract.. As directed
ECGC .... As directed
Cat's claw .... As directed
MSM .... As directed
Glucosmine sulfate .... As directed
Chondroitin .... As directed

Additional Therapies

AMMA™ therapy
Chiropractic manipulation
Massage therapy
Craniosacral therapy
Biofeedback
Reflexology
Kundalini breath work
Acupuncture/acupressure
Magnets

Fatigue Protocol

All protocols are to be used only with the professional guidance of a licensed dietician or clinician or physician.

In addition, the protocol does not infer to take all the supplements at one time. Rather it is meant to show all the supplements that have been shown to be beneficial for a condition. Therefore select 2–3 at a time.

Juicing Suggestions

- Two 6–12 oz green juices/day
- Three juices of lemon, lime, or watermelon diluted by 1 oz of lemon or lime, or 4 oz of watermelon with 12 oz of mineral water
- Add 2 oz aloe with each juice
- Include one grape juice (not white grapes) with seeds
- Add non-GMO soy isoflavone powder to one juice daily

Supplement Suggestions

Arabinogalactin	3 tbsp/day
L-Glutamine	1–5 g/day
Garlic	1,000 mg 2X/day
Aloe	3 oz 3X/day
St. John's wort extract	As directed
Evening Primrose oil	As directed
Curcumin	As directed
Echinacea extract	200 mg/day
Propolis	As directed

Plant-Sprout sterols/sitosterolins..............500 mg 4X/day
Astragalus.. As directed
Skullcap/Valerian .... As directed
Burdock/Red Clover/Dandelion .... As directed
Milk Thistle .... As directed
Pau d'arco.. As directed
Kombucha .... As directed
Cordyceps extract .... As directed
Nicotinamide riboside .... As directed
PQQ .... As directed
MGN 3 ....500 mg 3X/day
Pycnogenol .... As directed
Quercetin & bioflavonoids......................... 3,000 mg/day
Acidophilus .... As directed
Coenzyme Q10 ....300 mg 3 X/day
L-carnitine ....1,000 mg
Lecithin .... 1 tbsp 3 x/day
Manganese... 5 mg
Magnesium (from citrate)........................600 mg 2X/day
Digestive enzymes .... As directed
Vitamin A ....25,000 IU
Vitamin E .... 400–800 IU natural mixed tocopherols
DMG .... 100 mg 3 x/day
Vitamin B complex................................. 50 mg 2 x/day
Vitamin B12...1 mg methylated
GABA .... As directed
Ginseng .... As directed
Sea vegetable capsules .... As directed
Brain formula complex.............................. As directed
Anti-parasite formula .... As directed
Melatonin .... As directed

Food and Supplements

Food and Supplements

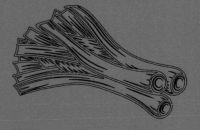

Organic Produce

All fruits and vegetables you eat should be organic, whenever possible, to avoid exposure to pesticides. There is certain conventionally grown produce that is especially risky to eat. According to the Environmental Working Group (EWG), a nonprofit environmental watchdog agency based in Washington, D.C., eating the twelve most contaminated conventionally grown fruits and vegetables would expose a person to nearly twenty pesticides per day on average. These foods are listed below (and are also listed on the EWG's website, at www.EWG.org). The website also lists the fifteen least contaminated fruits and vegetables; these foods are listed below as well.

"THE DIRTY DOZEN PLUS"

- apples
- celery
- lettuce
- grapes
- cucumbers
- nectarines (imported)
- peaches
- potatoes
- spinach
- strawberries
- sweet bell peppers
- cherry tomatoes
- snap peas

- hot peppers
- kale/collard greens

"THE CLEAN FIFTEEN"

- asparagus
- avocado
- papaya
- cauliflower
- kiwi
- grapefruit
- sweet potatoes
- mango
- onion
- pineapple
- sweet corn
- cabbage
- sweet peas
- eggplant
- cantaloupe (domestic)

Alkaline Foods

The vast majority of Americans consume an excess of acid-forming foods. Research has shown that tumor growth increases in an acid environment.[9,10,11] The blood is maintained in the body at a slightly alkaline level of between 7.2 and 7.4. Eating alkaline foods keeps the blood pH in its ideal range, which is important for the prevention and treatment of cancer. Ideally, the diet should consist of 80 percent alkaline-forming foods, such as those available from many raw fruits and vegetables, as well as nuts, seeds, grains, and legumes. What follows is a list of recommended alkaline-forming foods:

Fruits: Berries, apples, apricots, avocados, bananas, currants, dates, figs, grapefruit, grapes, kiwis, lemons, limes, mangoes, melons, nectarines, olives, oranges, papayas, peaches, pears, persimmons, pineapple, quince, raisins, raspberries, strawberries, tangerines, and watermelon.(The most alkaline-forming foods are lemons and melons.)

---

9 Smallbone, Kieran, et al. "The Role of Acidity in Solid Tumour Growth and Invasion." *Journal of Theoretical Biology* 235 (2005): 476-484.

10 Robey, Ian F., et al. "Bicarbonate Increases Tumor pH and Inhibits Spontaneous Metastases." *Cancer Research* 69, no. 2260 (2009). http://cancerres.aacrjournals.org/content/69/6/2260.abstract (accessed March 14, 2012).

11 Rofstad, Einar K., et al. "Acidic Extracellular pH Promotes Experimental Metastasis of Human Melanoma Cells in Athymic Nude Mice." *Cancer Research* 66 (2006). http://cancerres.aacrjournals.org/content/66/13/6699.abstract?ijkey=6f1de3d-cb24df43416f5003b8f892f1b6fd9d741&keytype2=tf_ipsecsha (accessed March 5, 2012).

Vegetables: Artichoke, asparagus, sprouts, beets, bell peppers, broccoli, Brussels sprouts, cabbage, carrots, cauliflower, celery, collards, corn, cucumbers, eggplant, endive, ginger, horseradish, kale, kelp, seaweeds, mustard greens, okra, onions, parsley, potatoes, radishes, spinach, squash, tomatoes, watercress, and yams.

Whole Grains: Amaranth, barley, oats, quinoa, and wild rice.

Beans/Legumes: Almonds, chestnuts, chickpeas, green beans, lima beans, peas, and soybeans.

Seeds: Alfalfa, chia, coconut, radish, and sesame.

Super Foods

Apples: For thousands of years, apples (*malus sylvestrsis*) have been used for a wide variety of medical complications and diseases, including diabetes, fevers, inflammatory conditions, and heart ailments. In addition to having confirmed many of the healthful properties of apples, modern research has identified invaluable phytochemicals contained by the fruits. Phytochemicals are chemical compounds that are found in plants and which have been used to treat illnesses. One of these found in apples is phloretin, a natural antibiotic. The fruits also contain pectin and pectic acids that provide essential bulk to a diet. The apple's tannins, quercetin, alpha-farnesene, shikimic acid, and chlorogenic acid also promote health benefits, such as increasing production of the neurotransmitter acetylcholine, so helping offset cognitive decline due to oxidative damage. With high levels of phenols, polyphenols, and other antioxidant, chemoprotective properties, apples have been shown to help guard against a variety of cancers, including leukemia and those that target the colon, lung, breast, liver, and skin. These apple's chemicals also provide essential nutrients to improve cardiovascular health, reduce the risk of coronary heart disease and stroke, and prevent atherosclerosis.

Apricots: This fruit had a long and rich history in the medical practices of China and India. In traditional Chinese medicine, apricots and their kernels are prescribed for treating asthma, cough, and constipation. The fruit is a stronghold of vitamins C and K, beta-carotene, thiamine, niacin, and iron. Japanese scientists have called attention to the apricot's ability to inhibit the pathogenic bacteria frequent in ulcers and acute gastritis.

Bananas: Bananas are low in calories while providing essential nutrients, among them vitamin B6, vitamin C, potassium, and manganese. They also stimulate probiotic activity, which sustains healthy gut flora. Bacteria in our gastrointestinal system are critical for proper digestion and absorption of nutrients. Bananas help keep this system on track. Recent findings have indicated that bananas may offer protection against kidney cancer, particularly in women, and aid renal function.

Blueberries: Many berries have health-boosting properties. Berries that are black, blue, and red are especially known for their possession of antioxidant nutrients. Blueberries specifically contain the antioxidant groups of flavonoids, phenolic and polyphenol compounds, all of which have shown some ability to reverse cellular aging of the cognitive and motor functions. The fruit's power was brought home in a recent study that compared the antioxidant levels of 100 different foods. Blueberries scored highest! Other examination have shown blueberries acting to protect brain health, improve memory, and sustain coordination by, for one, enhancing communication between nerve cells. This activity provides protection from serious neurodegenerative diseases, such as dementia and Alzheimer's. On top of this, blueberries have anti-inflammatory properties that protect the skin, joints, and the cardiovascular and neurological systems. Eating of the fruit has proven beneficial to those suffering from diabetes. It consumption prevents bone loss and inhibits cancer cell proliferation, particularly in the cases of prostate and colon cancer. With all these life-giving properties, blueberries have certainly earned the sobriquet "super food."

Broccoli: What makes broccoli a super food is its high concentration of the phytochemicals diindolymethane and isothiocyanate, which are powerful immunomodulators, that is, substances that have strong effects on the immune system. Because it fosters immune system strength, broccoli empowers that system in the fight against cancer (breast and prostate cancer, in particular) and provides protection from bacterial and viral infections. Along with the two aforementioned phytochemicals, broccoli also contains other anticancer agents, such as glucoraphanin. Due to these observed properties, right now a substantial amount of research is being conducted on broccoli's mutagenic qualities. This vegetable is rich in vitamins A, B5, B6, B9 (folate), C and K, and provides plenty of dietary fiber. It will also give anyone who eats it moderate amounts of calcium, iron, phosphorus, and potassium. As with other leafy green vegetables, it contains lutein and zeaxanthin, which foster eye health. Since it has more calcium than even most dairy products, it can protect bones and increase bone mass. Thus, it's another plant well deserving of its super food classification.

Carrots: Carrots can be looked to as chief provider of carotenoids, a family of antioxidants proven to block DNA and cellular membrane damage caused by free radical activity. This vegetable is rich in the phytochemicals alpha-carotene and lycopene, both shown to have anti-carcinogenic properties, fighting against cancer especially in the colon, lung, prostate, and stomach. The less-known black and purple carrots have high levels of anthocyanin, a powerful anti-cancer biochemical that studies have found slowing cancer cell proliferation by as much as 80 percent. Other work indicates the commonplace belief that carrots improve memory is far from mythical since the vegetable has shown capacity in boosting brain function. Add to that cardiovascular benefits, such as decreasing cholesterol. Another adage has it that carrots improve vision. This has been backed by the fact that carrots are high in retinoids that benefit ocular health. Since carrots are a good source of vitamin A, they should be kept in the diet of diabetics, given that A lowers blood sugar and aids in the development of insulin-producing cells in the pancreas. One cup of raw carrots can provide almost 700 percent of the daily recommended consumption of vitamin A and 220 percent of vitamin K, a substance critical for bone health. Thus, we have to dub carrots another superhero among edible plants.

Garlic: While garlic contains phytonutrients similar to those found in onions, it also possesses selenium, a substance that, according to some studies, offers protection against various cancers and against the deterioration of the body caused by free radicals. Different studies have looked at and remarked on its ability to both guard against heart disease and arterial calcification (hardening of the arteries), and to reduce cholesterol and blood pressure. Since it is a source of the flavonoid quercetin, it contains antibiotic properties that empower it to fight colds, stomach viruses, and yeast infections.

Ginger: Ginger is already widely employed throughout the world by anyone who wants to cure dyspepsia (stomach upsets), reduce gastrointestinal gases, and to relieve nausea that arises from pregnancy, seasickness, and even from chemo drugs used in cancer and other medical therapies. Ginger is largely composed of fragrant essential oils, which give it a distinctive aromatic flavor. One of these oils, gingerol, makes it a natural sedative for calming the gastrointestinal tract. This oil also provides some protection from pathogenic bacteria that upset the stomach. All in all, ginger is rich in antibiotic properties that combat the GI infections that bring on diarrhea and dehydration. Beyond this, new evidence suggests ginger helps lower cholesterol, a boon that provides protection from cardiovascular disease.

Folk medicine has long honored ginger. Bear in mind, by the way, that while some scientists look down on folk medicine, numerous modern pharmaceuticals have been derived from folk remedies, suitably renamed and price-tagged. This folk science, now supported by modern science, has seen ginger as a mild immune booster, which wards off colds and flus, sinus congestions, and coughs. There have also been some preliminary findings in animal studies suggesting that ginger may help to treat diabetes. This is an exciting new perspective.

Goji Berry: The goji berry, a fruit with many health-giving properties, has sometimes been traduced by more unscrupulous food companies by being sold in such things as (to imagine a name) "Goji Power Plus Bars," which are actually low on goji as an ingredient and high on unrefined sugar. Now let's look at the value of goji, which has caused such companies to try to trade on its good name. Also known as wolfberry in its native Europe, the plant is found through much of Asia, where it appears in exotic (to Westerners) Tibetan and Himalayan descriptions. The word goji is actually a Westernization of the Chinese word for the berry, which can be transliterated as "gouqi." The berry is a common ingredient in traditional Chinese medicine, dating back thousands of years in its use. The oblong red goji berry has no problem fulfilling the requirements to be designated a super food. It has a high concentration of phytochemicals, amino acids, vitamins B and C, and beta-carotene. Additionally, it contains 11 essential and 22 trace dietary minerals, is moderately high in alpha-linolenic acid, and an outstanding source of the antioxidant lycopene. One can look to the goji berry for extra protein, dietary fibers, calcium, zinc, and selenium. With all these nutrients found in it, the goji will obviously have many health-lifting effects, and these include protection from cardiovascular and inflammatory diseases as well as from age-related vision disorders (such as glaucoma and macular degeneration). Studies have pointed to its neuro-protection, positive immunomodulatory, and anti-cancer properties. This last benefit has been underscored by a study published in the *Chinese Journal of Oncology*, which indicated cancer patients responded better to treatment while on a diet that included goji. However, the study recommended that individuals on blood-thinning medications avoid eating goji berries, which may interfere with the drugs. Last but far from least, it offers liver protection and can improve sexual function.

Green Tea: The ingredient in tea—in green tea particularly—that has stirred the most scientific interest is catechin. Approximately 25 percent of a dry tea leaf is catechin. Although traces of catechin are also found in chocolate, wine, and other fruits and vegetables, it is tea that offers the greatest amount of this super nutrient. The multi-tasking catechin not only has been shown to reduce the plaque buildup that is part of atherosclerosis, but it gives protection against infectious bacteria, and reduces oxidative stress. In our polluted world, tea catechins are especially needed due to another of its curative features, which is that it can improve DNA replication and protect against genetic damage from environmental toxins. Studies in recent years have noted its inflammatory properties and suggested it can play a role battling against cancer. Other scientific examinations note that green tea can improve bone density and cognitive function, reduce the risk of developing kidney stones, and strengthen heart function. There is also some evidence showing that green tea's polyphenols protect against the brain cell death that is associated with Parkinson's and Alzheimer's diseases. I remember reading about the traditional Chinese dental hygiene procedure of brushing with tea. At the time, years ago, I thought it was humorous, but I realize now, that like many folk practices, it is rooted in real insight. Even if brushing with tea doesn't prevent cavities, it is full of other health enhancers.

Leafy Vegetables: Another "league of superheroes" among foods is found in the dark green leafy vegetables. This band includes spinach, kale, arugula, Swiss chard, cabbage, collard greens, and watercress. While they should be united in your diet, each eaten in turn, they all have individualized, singular health benefits. One thing they hold in common, however, is that they are high in carotenoids and other antioxidants that guard against heart disease, cancer, and problems in blood sugar regulation. To choose one example from among them, one cup of cooked kale provides over 1,300 percent of the daily requirement of vitamin K needed for maximum bone health. It is also rich in calcium and manganese, other nurturers of bone density. Like broccoli, kale contains the anti-cancer phytochemical sulforaphane. To note the value of a few more of the green leafy vegetables, look at cabbage, which contains manifold glutamine, an amino acid that contributes to the anti-inflammatory activities in the body. This acid also protects from infectious complications due to human papilloma virus (HPV). The juice from cabbage will quicken the healing of peptic ulcers. Now, turn to spinach. It is one of the best sources for iron. Per gram, it generally contains over 30 percent more iron than a hamburger. (Any diet heavy in spinach should include sufficient vitamin C to help assimilate the iron.) Spinach is also an excellent source of folic acid, calcium, copper, zinc, selenium, and omega-3 fatty acids. Although I can't give details on every green leafy vegetable, let me end with two more. Watercress is a superb source of phytochemicals. It has been shown to be a diuretic and digestive aid as well as an aid in protecting against lung cancer and strengthening the thyroid. Collard greens supply ample quantities of immune response modulator diindolylmethane.

Legumes: The modern Western diet, especially in America, ignores most legumes at its detriment. Sometimes I think the only way that Americans would take to legumes would be if they came in a hamburger bun and were sloshed with ketchup and mustard. But, to be more serious, when I mention legumes, most people think of beans, peas, and lentils. However, alfalfa, clover, peanuts, and cashews are also legumes. These vegetables and grains are excellent sources of cholesterol lowering fiber. When you consume a legume, its fiber content helps you manage blood sugar levels. One cup of lentils can provide upwards to 65 percent of the minimum, daily necessary dietary fiber. With this high fiber content in a serving, when legumes are frequently included in meals, we are assured to have better gastrointestinal and colon health. Legumes in general contain energy-boosting protein and iron. Looking at specific entities in this group, black beans are rich in the potent antioxidant anthocyanidins, which promotes heart and vascular health. Green beans are excellent sources of vitamins C and K. Garbanzo beans, commonly known as chickpeas, are a superb source of molybdenum, which strengthens teeth and preserves tooth enamel. Another important legume that is not as familiar in the US as some of those just mentioned is the adzuki bean. Originally from the Himalayas and standard in East Asian cooking, they are a rich source of magnesium, potassium, iron, zinc, and B vitamins. Very high in soluble fiber, the adzuki helps eliminate bad cholesterol from the body. In Japan, it is treasured for its kidney and bladder health-promoting function, and used in weight-loss programs. To maximize the benefits of legumes in the diet, combine them with whole grains. The reason for this recommendation is that legumes are very low in methionine, an essential amino acid that supports cellular life, while whole grains are replete with this amino acid, but low in lysine, which is abundant in legumes. A wholesome, integrated vegetarian diet will contain a balance of legumes and grains.

Mushrooms: My friends, who have travelled to the Yunnan province in China, mention how there some of the most prized edibles are the wide varieties of mushrooms. Where an average, un-health-conscious American would find his or her greatest culinary delight in choosing between cuts of steak, the Yunnan citizen is delicately discriminating between different mushrooms. A wealth of growing peer-reviewed science, which would recommend the Yunnan culinary emphasis, shows that many edible mushrooms are among the more important immune builders in the plant kingdom. In particular, medicinal mushrooms inhibit tumor growth, have anti-pathogenic and blood-sugar-lowering activities, and strengthen immunity. Among approximately 200 different varieties whose health-enhancing skills have been noted are the chaga, cordyceps, maitake, oyster, portobello, reishi, shiitake, and turkey tail mushrooms. Although it is possible to find all of these in fresh or dried form, at the moment in the US the shiitake mushrooms are the easiest to obtain. A list of the benefits obtained from mushrooms would have to mention their antiviral and antibacterial properties, which in different mushrooms have shown some effectiveness against a wide spread of pathogens, including those from polio, hepatitis B, influenza, candida, Epstein-Barr virus, streptococcus, and tuberculosis. The mutagenic benefits of mushrooms that one can read about in the scientific literature note how mushrooms can be enlisted in the fight against leukemia, sarcoma, and the bladder, breast, colon, liver, lung, prostate, and stomach cancers, even in advanced stages.

Onions: A rule of thumb is that the more pungent the onion, the greater its health benefits. It's as if you could smell its disease-thwarting power. Onions are particularly important to include in diets for diabetics, for one, because they are rich in chromium, a trace mineral that helps cells respond to insulin. Moreover, refined sugar depletes the body's chromium levels, so for anyone that has this sugar in his or her diet, onions are an excellent source of replacement. Onions are also rich in vitamin B6, vitamin C, manganese, molybdenum (essential in preserving tooth enamel), potassium, phosphorous, and copper. They are also just about the best source of quercetin, which works hand-in-hand with vitamin C in help the body eliminate bacteria and strengthen immunity. The onion's health benefits don't stop there. Inclusion of onions in the diet help individuals lower blood pressure and cholesterol, and strengthen bone health. Onions also have anti-inflammatory benefits, reducing symptoms related to inflammatory conditions, such as asthma, arthritis, and respiratory congestion. Some studies have noted that they lessen the adverse effects from colds and flus.

Oranges: The orange is a vitamin and mineral-packed treasure chest of a fruit, rich in vitamins A, B and C, potassium, and calcium, as well as being an excellent source of fiber. One phytonutrient in oranges that boosts it into the super food category is the flavonoid hesperidin. This biochemical works to support healthy blood vessels and reduces cholesterol. What has been established so far overlooks what the public considers the orange's defining health trait, it being stocked with vitamin C, an important antioxidant that limits free radicals while also building the immune system. Vitamin C's healing properties are well known and have been repeatedly scientifically validated. These include the lessening of arterial plaque as well as protecting from Alzheimer's, Parkinson's, and Crohn's diseases, arthritis, and diabetes.

Peppers (capsicum): Native American folk medicine, which has so many features we can still learn from, gave a prominent place in its pharmacology to peppers of the capsicum family, which includes bell and chili peppers. Recent work suggests that the nutrient capsaicin, found in these peppers, is a natural analgesic and a neuro-inflammatory blocker that relieves aches and pains to joints and muscles. This is one reason why Native American medicine prescribed a topical application of pepper to painful areas of the body. Capsaicin is particularly deserving of mention in this book because recent, promising research in Canada has explored the uses of capsaicin in the treatment of Type I diabetes. Other work has noted it can benefit sufferers from prostate cancer and leukemia. Some scientists have noted that this much studied nutrient found in peppers helps with weight loss, stimulation of insulin-producing cells, and prevention of LDL cholesterol oxidation. Another benefit recently uncovered is that the nutrient protects from stomach ulcerations and induces apoptosis (cancer cell death) in lung cancer. Setting aside the value of capsaicin, peppers can also be prized because they are rich in the antioxidant vitamins A as well as in vitamins B1, B6, E, and K. They are also high in potassium, magnesium, and iron. Yellow peppers are rich in lutein and zeaxanthin, which protect from eye disease and blindness.

Soy: Comparative studies that have considered dietary reasons for the lower cancer rates in the East as compared to the West always point to soy as one of the major foods that distinguish these global eating patterns and so may have something to do with lower cancer rates. Scientists have taken this suggestion and done a number of studies that give evidence that the phytochemicals in soy protect against the genesis of cancer. Isoflavones, including genistein and daidzein, that are major constituents in soy, seem to be some of the active ingredients that provide natural protection against various cancers: breast, colon, endometrial, and prostate. One important Japanese study involving over 24,000 women found those who had the highest soy content in their diet were best protected against breast cancer. A later Japanese study noted the soy isoflavones could reduce breast cancer risk by up to 54 percent. Along with this exciting attribute, soy has given evidence of an ability to lower blood LDL cholesterol and promote good HDL cholesterol, improve cardiac function, strengthen bone mass, and stabilize blood sugar. In vegetarian diets, soy-based foods are an excellent replacement for animal protein. Soybeans are also high in iron, omega-3 fatty acids, phosphorus, riboflavin, magnesium, and potassium.

Tomatoes: You have probably gotten the idea by now that one thing that distinguishes super foods from other eatables is that they contain very potent organic compounds, such a phytochemicals, that boost their health giving propensities. Tomatoes are no exception. They are the best source for lycopene, a carotenoid biochemical that gives tomatoes their red color, and is packed with positive properties. It has been estimated that approximately 80 percent of the lycopene consumed in the US derives from tomatoes and tomato-based foods. There is a vast body of scientific literature confirming lycopene's antioxidant and anti-mutagenic properties. This chemical is noteworthy for its protection against and treatment of various cancers, running the gamut from bladder, breast, cervix, lungs, and mouth to ovarian, prostate, and stomach cancer. Because diabetics often have low levels of lycopene in their blood, tomatoes should become a regular part of their diets. Tomatoes have been shown to prevent cholesterol oxidation, lower blood pressure, and decrease the risk of atherosclerosis. Other benefits that may accrue to the eater of these plants is improved renal function. Tomatoes also have antiviral and antibacterial qualities. In particular, lycopene can protect against human papilloma virus, one pathogen that has been associated with cancer. Tomatoes are also rich in most of the B complex vitamins as well as in potassium, manganese, chromium, folate, and iron. You can look to the tomato as an excellent source of the amino acid tryptophan, which is important for neurological health and can improve sleep.

Whole Grains: By now most Americans are aware that whole grain breads and pastas are healthier than those made from white flour, and brown rice is higher in nutrients and health benefits than white rice. However, once a person has changed over to brown rice and whole grain breads, he or she still has a rich world of whole grains to explore, each of which offers unique health benefits and phyto-nutrients. As with legumes, whole grains are rich in fiber. Take spelt, which is being used in breads and pastas and will provide 75 percent of the recommended daily requirement for vitamin B2. Spelt is highly water soluble, which means its nutrients are easily absorbed. There is evidence that spelt is a good choice for diabetics. Another grain, barley, is distinguished by being an excellent source of selenium, a substance that reduces the risk of colon disorders and colorectal cancer. Because barley is high in tryptophan, it will aid in sleep regulation. A third important grain, millet, is high in manganese, magnesium, and phosphorous, all of which support cardiovascular health. You are probably familiar with the grains I've just mentioned, but two that you may not have been alerted to are kamut and quinoa. The Glycemic Research Institute in Washington, D.C., has trumpeted the value of kamut for its low-glycemic properties, which makes it an ideal super food for diabetics, athletes, and people suffering from obesity. It is also an excellent substitute for those with wheat allergies, giving them the benefit of its possessing 65 percent more amino acids than wheat. Quinoa has been identified as a super food among grains for its ability to balance blood sugar and provide high quality fiber and protein to the diet. It is higher in calcium, phosphorus, iron, and zinc than are wheat, barley, and corn. In addition to balancing insulin resistance, quinoa is one of the most complete foods in nature, earning its super food status not only by the aforementioned traits but because it protects against atherosclerosis and breast cancer, and acts as a probiotic to foster the good micro-flora in the gut.

Cancer Fighting Foods

In addition to balancing the body's pH through a mostly alkaline diet, the following foods stand out as beneficial in preventing and treating cancer:

Cruciferous vegetables: Vegetables in the cruciferous family include kale, cabbage, broccoli, cauliflower, arugula, watercress, turnips, mustard plant, Brussels sprouts, and bokchoy. Cruciferous vegetables contain detoxifying compounds called indoles and isothiocyanates, which have been proven to help prevent and reverse cancer.[12,13,14,15] Recent research has identified sulforaphane, a compound found in broccoli, cabbage, and other cruciferous vegetables as a potent anticancer agent.[16] Packed with

---

12 Cover, C. M., et al. (1998). Indole-3-Carbinol Inhibits the Expression of Cyclin-Dependent Kinase-6 and Induces a G1 Cell Cycle Arrest of Human Breast Cancer Cells Independent of Estrogen Receptor Signaling. *J BiolChem* 273:3838-47.

13 Chen, I., et al. (1996). Indole-3-Carbinol and Diindolylmethane as Aryl Hydrocarbon (Ah) Receptor Agonists and Antagonists in T47D Human Breast Cancer Cells. *BiochemPharmacol* 51:1069-76.

14 Verhagen H., et al. (1995). Reduction of Oxidative DNA-Damage in Humans by Brussels Sprouts. *Carcinogenesis* 16:969-70.

15 Verhoeven D. T., et al. (1996). Epidemiological Studies on Brassica Vegetables and Cancer Risk. *Cancer Epidemiol Biomarkers Prev* 733-48.

16 "Discovery May Help Scientists Boost Broccoli's Cancer-Fighting Power." EurekAlert!. http://www.eurekalert.org/pub_releases/2010-10/uoic-dmh102110.php (accessed March 2, 2012).

raw and all-natural kale, broccoli, Brussels sprouts, and other cruciferous vegetables, cruciferous powders can offer a rich source of anticancer nutrition.

Green Foods: Wheatgrass, barley grass, alfalfa, blue-green algae, arugula, spinach, chlorella and spirulina, and other green foods are rich in blood-purifying chlorophyll and other important phytonutrients for detoxifying the system and rejuvenating organs. Laboratory tests have established that chlorophyll inhibits the activity of carcinogens at a molecular level.[17] Studies have demonstrated the capacity of chlorophyll-rich foods to reduce tumor growth[18,19,20] Containing spinach, chlorella, spirulina, barley grass juice powder, and fifteen other detoxifying vegetables, certain green powders are loaded with phytonutrients proven to be highly beneficial in cancer prevention and healing.

Red Foods: Research confirms that red foods such as strawberries, tomatoes, raspberries, pomegranates, tart cherries, cranberries, and goji berries are high in immunosupportive and cancer-fighting nutrients such as lycopene and

---

17   "Chlorophyll and Chlorophyllin." Linus Pauling Institute at Oregon State University. http://lpi.oregonstate.edu/infocenter/phytochemicals/chlorophylls/index.html#biological_activity (accessed January 3, 2012).

18   Cha, K. H., S. Y. Koo, and D. U. Lee. "AntiproliferativeEffects of Carotenoids Extracted from Chlorella ellipsoidea and Chlorella vulgaris on Human Colon Cancer Cells." *Journal of Agricultural and Food Chemistry* 56, no. 22 (2008): 10521-6.

19   Mathew, B., R. Sankaranarayanan, P. P. Nair, C. Varghese, T. Somanathan, B. P. Amma., N. S. Amma, and M. K. Nair. "Evaluation of Chemoprevention of Oral Cancer with SpirulinaFusiformis." *Nutrition and Cancer* 1995; 24(2):197-202.

20   Maeda, N., et al. "Anti-Cancer Effect of Spinach Glycoglycerolipids as Angiogenesis Inhibitors Based on the Selective Inhibition of DNA Polymerase Activity." *Mini Reviews in Medicinal Chemistry* 11 (2011). http://www.ncbi.nlm.nih.gov/pubmed/21034405 (accessed March 3, 2012).

carotene.[21,22,23] Many red foods also have high antioxidant content, making them an integral component of any anticancer diet. The antioxidant power of raspberries, strawberries, pomegranate, and dozens of other nutrient-rich fruits make some red and berry powders cancer superfoods.

Fiber: Though not a food itself, fiber is an important component of fruits, vegetables, and whole grains. The typical American diet includes about 14 g of fiber each day, which falls short of what is necessary for cancer prevention. Studies have indicated that 30 g of dietary fiber daily decrease the risk of colorectal cancer. Research has also suggested that high fiber intake may lower the risk of breast, colorectal, uterine, and prostate cancers.[24,25,26]

Olive Oil: Olive oil has been shown to possess anticancer properties. Studies have demonstrated that the monounsaturated fatty acids contained in olive

21 Blot, W. J, J. Y. Li, P. R. Taylor, et al. "Nutrition Intervention Trials in Linxian, China: Supplementation with Specific Vitamin/Mineral Combinations, Cancer Incidence, and Disease-Specific Mortality in the General Population." *J Natl Cancer Inst* 1993;85:1483–91.

22 Tanaka, T., M. Shminimizu, and H. Moriwaki. "Cancer Chemoprevention by Carotenoids." *Molecules* 14;17, no. 3 (2012): 3202-42. http://www.ncbi.nlm.nih.gov/pubmed/22418926 (accessed March 27, 2012).

23 Pinela, J. et al. "Nutritional Composition and Antioxidant Activity of Four Tomato (Lycopersiconesculentum L.) Farmer' Varieties in Northeastern Portugal Home Gardens." *Food and Chemical Toxicology* 50, no. (3-4) (2011): 829-34.

24 "Fiber." University of Maryland Medical Center. http://www.umm.edu/altmed/articles/fiber-000303.htm (accessed December 3, 2012).

25 HealthDay. "High-Fiber Diet May Thwart Colon Cancer." USATODAY.com. http://yourlife.usatoday.com/health/medical/cancer/story/2011-11-11/High-fiber-diet-may-help-thwart-colon-cancer/51168932/1 (accessed March 28, 2012).

26 "Uterine Cancer—2—Endometrial Cancer, Vitamin A, Vitamin C—Life Extension Health Concern." Life Extension. http://www.lef.org/protocols/cancer/uterine_cancer_02.htm (accessed March 28, 2012).

oil have a protective effect against cancer growth.[27,28] Research has also shown that the phytochemicals abundant in olive oil inhibit cancer growth in vitro.[29] But remember, more isn't always better. Olive oil still has 120 calories per tablespoon, so don't go overboard. For maximum benefit, olive oil should be used in moderation. Choose a good-quality, extra virgin, cold-pressed variety.

Juices: Freshly squeezed fruit and vegetable juices provide valuable enzymes and antioxidant nutrients that are easily digestible. Compounds in cabbage juice have been observed to have favorable effects on stomach and colorectal cancer.[30,31] Rich in beta-carotene and vitamin A, carrot juice is beneficial but should be watered down, as it is also high in sugar, and can potentially spike blood sugar levels.[32] Adding a teaspoon of vitamin C to juices creates an even more potent preventive tonic.

---

27 Owen, R. W., R. Haubner, G. Wurtele, E. Hull, B. Spiegelhalder, and H. Bartsch. "Olives and Olive Oil in Cancer Prevention." *Eur J Cancer Prev.* 2004 Aug;13(4):319-26.

28 Menendez, J. A., and R. Lupu. "Mediterranean Dietary Traditions for the Molecular Treatment of Human Cancer: Anti-oncogenic Actions of the Main Olive Oil's Monounsaturated Fatty Acid Oleic Acid (18:1n-9)." *Curr Pharm Biotechnol.* 2006 Dec;7(6):495-502.

29 Menendez, Javier A., Alejandro Vazquez-Martin, Rocio Garcia-Villalba, Alegria Carrasco-Pancorbo, Cristina Oliveras-Ferraros, Alberto Fernandez-Gutierrez, and Antonio Segura-Carretero. "Anti-HER2 (erbB-2) Oncogene Effects of Phenolic Compounds Directly Isolated from Commercial Extra-Virgin Olive Oil (EVOO)." *BMC Cancer.2008 Dec 18;8:377.*

30 Choi, Hyun Ju, Do Young Lim, and Jung Han Yoon Park. "Induction of G1 and G2/M Cell Cycle Arrests by the Dietary Compound 3,3'-diindolylmethane in HT-29 Human Colon Cancer Cells." *BMC Gastroenterology* 9, no. 39 (2009).

31 Bhatnagar, N. "3,3'-diindolylmethane Enhances the Efficacy of Butyrate in Colon Cancer Prevention through Down-Regulation of Survivin." *Cancer Prevention Research* 2, no. 6 (2009): 581-9.

32 Schnäbele, K., et al. "Effects of Carrot and Tomato Juice Consumption on FaecalMarkers Relevant to Colon Carcinogenesis in Humans." *The British Journal of Nutrition* 99, no. 3 (2008): 606-613. http://www.ncbi.nlm.nih.gov/pubmed/18254985 (accessed March 13, 2012).

Green Tea: High in antioxidants known as polyphenoliccatechins, green tea has been shown to help prevent skin, lung, esophageal, stomach, pancreatic, and bladder cancer in animals.[33] Studies have demonstrated that green tea extract halts the spread of chronic lymphocytic leukemia.[34] Recent research also indicates that green tea contains compounds that considerably slow the growth of cancer cells.[35]

Mushrooms: Several varieties of mushrooms have powerful healing properties. The maitake mushroom kills cancer cells by enhancing the activity of T-helper cells.[36] Research has shown the maitake mushroom to exert a favorable effect on various types of cancer, including breast, colon, and prostate.[37,38,39] Both shiitake and reishi mushrooms have also been

33   "Tea." Linus Pauling Institute at Oregon State University. http://lpi.oregonstate.edu/infocenter/phytochemicals/tea/ (accessed January 3, 2012).

34   "Green Tea Extract Appears to Keep Cancer in Check in Majority of CLL Patients." Mayo Clinic. http://www.mayoclinic.org/news2010-rst/5833.html (accessed January 3, 2012).

35   E. J. Okello, G. J. McDougall, S. Kumar, and C. J. Seal. "In Vitro Protective Effects of Colon-Available Extract of Camellia sinensis (Tea) against Hydrogen Peroxide and Beta-amyloid (Aβ(1–42)) Induced Cytotoxicity in Differentiated PC12 Cells." *Phytomedicine*, 2010; DOI:10.1016/j.phymed.2010.11.004

36   Yeh, Jan-Ying, et al. "Antioxidant Properties and Antioxidant Compounds of Various Extracts from the Edible BasidiomyceteGrifolaFrondosa (Maitake)." *Molecules* 16, no. 4 (2011): 3197-3211.

37   Chan, J. Y., et al. "Enhancement of In Vitro and In Vivo Anticancer Activities of Polysaccharide Peptide from Grifolafrondosa by Chemical Modifications." *Pharmaceutical Biology* 49, no. 11 (2011): 1114-1120

38   Masuda, Y. "A Polysaccharide Extracted from Grifolafrondosa Enhances the Anti-tumor Activity of Bone Marrow-Derived Dendritic Cell-Based Immunotherapy against Murine Colon Cancer." *Cancer Immunology, Immunotherapy* 59, no. 10 (2009): 1531-41.

39   Fullerton, S. A. "Induction of Apoptosis in Human Prostatic Cancer Cells with Beta-glucan (MaitakeMushroom Polysaccharide)." *Molecular Urology* 4, no. 1 (2000): 7-13.

observed to have strong antitumor properties in animals.[40,41,42] Research has revealed that the cordyceps mushroom inhibits the division and proliferation of cancer cells.[43] And, surprisingly, the common white button mushroom has been shown to suppress aromatase activity and estrogen biosynthesis, which make it an excellent breast cancer chemopreventive agent.[44]

Macrobiotic Foods: Proponents of macrobiotic eating claim that cancer patients following this approach lead longer and better-quality lives. In several cases, cancer patients deemed incurable by mainstream medicine have reported full recoveries on a macrobiotic diet. Success may be due to high levels of antioxidant nutrients and a low amount of fat. In fact, the total percentage of calories from fat in macrobiotic diets is approximately 10 to 12 percent, a 30 percent drop from the average American diet. Best results with the macrobiotic diet are seen with endocrine-related cancers, such as cancer of the breast, prostate, pancreas, uterus and ovaries. This is because with these cancers, too many fat cells produce or synthesize estrogen and androgen hormones that contribute to the disease; reducing the amount of dietary fat lessens hormone production.

40 Tanaka, K., et al. "Oral Ingestion of LentinulaedodesMycelia Extract Inhibits B16 Melanoma Growth via Mitigation of Regulatory T Cell-Mediated Immunosuppression." *Cancer Science* 102, no. 3 (2011): 516-21.

41 Israilides, C., et al. "In Vitro Cytostatic and Immunomodulatory Properties of the Medicinal Mushrooms Lentinula Edodes." *Phytomedicine,* June 2008.

42 Sliva, Daniel. "Ganoderma Lucidum(Reishi) in Cancer Treatment." *Integrative Cancer Therapies* 2, no. 4 (2003): 358-364.

43 Das, Shonkor Kumar, et al.; "Medicinal Uses of the Mushroom Cordyceps Militaris: Current State and Prospects." *Fitoterapia,* December 2010.

44 Chen S. et al, Anti-aromatase activity of phytochemicals in white button mushrooms, *Cancer Research,* December 15, 2006, 2006;66:12026-12034.

Seaweeds: Chinese medicine has long recognized the value of seaweed for treating cancers, as it softens hardened tumors. More recently, research has shed light on the powerful mix of micronutrients, including Vitamin C and Vitamin E, as well as minerals, iodine, fiber, and polysaccharides in seaweed, which make it a powerful nutritional tool in combating cancer.[45,46] Considered to be one of the healthiest people on earth, the Japanese consume more seaweed than any other nation.

Spices: Spices offer numerous health-promoting benefits, and certain spices have been found to aid in the prevention and treatment of cancer. Research has associated black pepper and cumin intake with a lower incidence of colon cancer.[47,48,49] Rosemary is known to help prevent DNA damage by

45   Burtin, Patricia. "Nutritional Value of Seaweed." *Electronic Journal of Environmental and Food Chemistry Agricultural* 2 (2003). http://ejeafche.uvigo.es/index.php?option=com_docman&task=doc_view&gid=208 (accessed January 3, 2012).

46   Ermakova, S., et al. "Fucoidansfrom Brown Seaweeds Sargassumhornery, Ecloniacava, Costariacostata: Structural Characteristics and Anticancer Activity." *Applied Biochemistry and Biotechnology,*; July 2011.

47   Gali-Muhtasib, H., M. Diab-Assaf, C. Boltze, J. Al-Hmaira, R. Hartig, etal." Thymoquinone Extracted from Black Seed Triggers Apoptotic Cell Death in Human Colorectal Cancer Cells Via a p53-dependent Mechanism." *International Journal of Oncology,* October 2004.

48   Salim, E. I., and S. Fukushima." Chemopreventive Potential of Volatile Oil from Black Cumin (Nigella sativa L.) Seeds against Rat Colon Carcinogenesis." *Nutrition and Cancer,* 2003.

49   S. Duessel, et al. "Growth Inhibition of Human Colon Cancer Cells by Plant Compounds." *Clinical Laboratory Science,* 2008.

carcinogens and suppress cancer cell proliferation.[50,51,52] Capsaicin, an ingredient found in chili peppers, kills prostate cancer cells.[53] Evidence suggests that parsley combats lung and breast cancer.[54,55]

50   Chan, M. M., C. T. Ho, and H. I. Huang. "Effects of Three Dietary Phytochemicals from Tea, Rosemary and Turmeric on Inflammation-Induced Nitrite Production." *Cancer Letters* 96:23-29, 1995.

51   S. Cheung, et al. "Anti-proliferative and Antioxidant Properties of Rosemary Rosmarinus Officinalis." *Oncology Reports*, June 2007.

52   Ho, C. H., T. Ferraro, et al. "Phytochemicals in Tea and Rosemary and Their Cancer-Preventive Properties." In Ho, C. T., T. Osawa, et al., eds., *Food Phytochemicals for Cancer Prevention II*:2-19. Washington, DC: American Chemical Society, 1994.

53   "Pepper Component Hot Enough to Trigger Suicide in Prostate Cancer Cells." Cedars-Sinai Hospital. http://www.cedars-sinai.edu/About-Us/News/News-Releases-2006/Pepper-Component-Hot-Enough-To-Trigger-Suicide-In-Prostate-Cancer-Cells 15 Mar, 2006.

54   Johnson, J. J. "Carnosol: A Promising Anti-cancer and Anti-inflammatory Agent." *Cancer Letters* 305, no. 1 (2011): 1-7. http://www.ncbi.nlm.nih.gov/pubmed/21382660 (accessed March 12, 2012).

55   "Parsley, Celery Carry Crucial Component for Fight against Breast Cancer, Study Suggests." Science Daily. http://www.sciencedaily.com/releases/2011/05/110509122732.htm (accessed March 21, 2012).

Supplements

The value of antioxidants, particularly beta-carotene; vitamins A, C, and E; flavonoids; selenium; glutathione; superoxide dismutase; and coenzyme Q10 cannot be overestimated in disease fighting and prevention. Antioxidants attack free radicals before they do irrevocable damage. Many clinical studies confirm their protective effects, while other research shows that antioxidants increase a patient's tolerance of chemotherapy and radiation.

Aloe Vera: Aloe vera, which many people will recognize as an additive to natural shampoos and skincare products, also has been shown to play a role in fighting diabetes. Studies indicate that it can lower glucose among type II diabetics. A particularly illuminating investigation reported that aloe vera, given to non-insulin dependent diabetics over a 14-week period, reduced blood sugar levels by 45 percent, on average.

Alpha-Lipoic Acid: This is a powerful antioxidant that neutralizes the hydroxyl radical (which plays a role in all stages of cancer growth) as well as other free radicals. It boosts glutathione, which combats the damaging cytokines, and regenerates vitamins C and E and coenzyme Q10. Further, alpha-lipoic acid has been shown to activate the anticancer caspase enzyme, induce cancer cell apoptosis, and suppress metastasis.[56,57,58] Like garlic, alpha lipoic acid combats many of the negative accompaniments of diabetes. It positively affects the control of blood sugar, lowering blood sugar levels, while helping fight off the development of long-term complications that can damage the heart and kidneys. As an antioxidant, it kills free radicals, helping to reduce pain, burning, itching, tingling and numbness in people who have nerve damage caused by diabetes (called peripheral neuropathy). This last facet of the substance was established by a study that indicated treating diabetics with 600 mg/day of alpha lipoic acid for three weeks significantly reduced the symptoms of diabetic peripheral neuropathy. Lipoic acid also reduces fat accumulation, which will forestall the acquisition of diabetes in the first place.

Beta-Carotene: The liver converts beta-carotene to vitamin A as needed, making it a safe source of the vitamin, especially for women of childbearing years, as no fetal problems are associated with it. (Note: People with liver problems may be unable to convert beta-carotene into vitamin A.) In addition, beta-carotene itself stimulates T-helper cells, which prevent the development of cancer. Further studies have demonstrated beta-carotene protects against lung and colon cancer. Fifty thousand international units taken daily may prevent cancer in cigarette smokers.

Bilberry Extract: As with ginkgo, bilberry extract has been given a trial of its healing components with both animal and human subjects. Diabetic mice given a herbal extract with bilberry showed a significant lowering of

---

56 van de Mark, K, et al. "Alpha-lipoic Acid Induces p27Kip-Dependent Cell Cycle Arrest in Non-transformed Cell Lines and Apoptosis in Tumor Cell Lines." *Journal of Cellular Physiology* 194, no. 3 (2003): 325-40.

57 Lee, H. S., et al.; "Alpha-Lipoic Acid Reduces Matrix Metalloproteinase Activity in MDA-MB-231 Human Breast Cancer Cells." *Nutrition Research,* 2010.

58 Myzak, M. C., and A. C. Carr. "Myeloperoxidase-Dependent Caspase-3 Activation and Apoptosis in HL-60 Cells: Protection by the Antioxidants Ascorbate and (Dihydro)lipoic Acid." *Redox Report* 7, no. 1 (2002): 47-53. http://www.ncbi.nlm.nih.gov/pubmed/11981455 (accessed March 13, 2012).

their blood glucose. Humans with retinopathy (damage to the retina often caused by diabetes), who as part of a scientific study were given bilberry, were found to have decreased vascular permeability (blood leaking from the vessels) and reduced hemorrhage.

Biotin: As we've seen, diabetics have trouble moving glucose out of the blood into storage places in the cells. One place where glucose is kept is the liver. Here is where biotin comes in. Biotin boosts insulin sensitivity and increases the activity of the enzyme responsible for the first step in the utilization of glucose by the liver. This and other values of the vitamin have been shown in experiments on animals that indicate a high biotin diet may improve glucose tolerance and enhance insulin secretion.

Bitter Melon: Another all-purpose agent is bitter melon. In this case, it is not that it combats so many connected diseases, but that it works on both type I (insulin dependent) and type II (adult-onset) diabetes. For type II sufferers, bitter melon works by reducing insulin resistance, but it is beneficial to diabetics of both types due to its ability to lower and maintain proper levels of blood sugar.

Boron: Boron should be taken during and after menopause, as research shows it to be a precursor of hormones in both men and women.

Calcium: As you likely already know, calcium is essential for bone health and can help prevent osteoporosis. Calcium exists in many forms, and should be taken long before the onset of menopause. While dairy contains some calcium, there are healthier and more absorbable sources of this essential mineral. These sources include calcium citrate, which is easy to digest; calcium carbonate, which is alkaline and more difficult to digest; amino acid chelate, which is particularly strong; calcium lactate; and calcium gluconate, which comes in powdered form and can be mixed into beverages.

Calcium Citrate: Another chemical, calcium citrate, which is a form of citric acid, is, like vitamin E, of value in reducing the likelihood of becoming diabetic. Scientists have found that the high intake of calcium citrate along with vitamin D3, and vitamin D3 especially from supplementation, can decrease the risk of diabetes by 33 percent.

Carnosine: The antioxidant carnosine inhibits glycation, which we've seen disables proteins, and has demonstrated protective effects against diabetes-induced kidney damage.

Carotenoids: Carotenoids are the naturally occurring pigments found in various plants. With oncology, mixed carotenoids are important as free radical scavengers.[59,60] Lycopene is associated with low risk of breast, prostate, lung, and colon cancers.[61] There is an inverse relationship between beta-carotene and thyroid carcinoma. Lutein offers protection against breast cancer in premenopausal women.[62,63] Suggested doses are 9 to 20 mg of sulforaphane, 10 to 30 mg of lycopene, and 15 to 40 mg of lutein, along with a mixed carotenoid blend containing alpha- and beta-carotene.

Chromium Picolinate: Chromium is an essential trace mineral that plays a major role in moving glucose through its metabolic processes, which include being broken down from an ingested food and transferred to a cell. Scientific studies have shown that chromium picolinate helps people with type II diabetes control blood sugar levels and enhances use of proteins,

59 Ruano-Ravina, A., A. Figueiras, and J. M. Barros-Dios. "Diet and Lung Cancer: A New Approach." *Eur J Cancer Prev* 2000;9:395-400.

60 DiGiovanna, J. J. "Retinoid Chemoprevention in Patients at High Risk for Skin Cancer." *Med Pediatr Oncol* 2001;36:564-7.

61 Null, Gary. *The Complete Encyclopedia of Natural Healing*. New York: Kensington, 1998.

62 E. Cho et al. "Premenopausal Intakes of Vitamins A, C, and E, Folate, and Carotenoids, and Risk of Breast Cancer." *Cancer Epidemiology, Biomarkers and Prevention,* August 2003.

63 Zhang, Shumin, et al. "Dietary Carotenoids and Vitamins A, C, and E and Risk of Breast Cancer." *Journal of the National Cancer Institute,* 1999.

carbohydrates, and lipids. Given in higher doses, it aids such patients by increasing insulin sensitivity, which helps glucose enter cells and so lowers blood sugar levels.

Cinnamon Extract: As with quite a number of the supplements profiled already in this protocol, a well-known substance, here cinnamon, contains within its chemical architecture one or more vital, health-enhancing substances. A study performed at the US Department of Agriculture's Beltsville Human Nutrition Research Center isolated insulin-enhancing complexes in cinnamon. These are involved in preventing or alleviating glucose intolerance and diabetes. Once again something from the plant world—cinnamon is obtained from bark—is revealing more about nature's medical bounty.

Coenzyme Q10: Coenzyme Q10 (CoQ10), like vitamin C, is another miracle worker. It is something of a Renaissance chemical in that it not only helps control blood sugar, but decreases blood pressure and reduces oxidative damage that is the result of diabetes. Coenzyme Q10 works in conjunction with other enzymes in the body to optimize energy. Specifically, Q10 improves oxygen utilization, acts as a stimulus to the immune system, and serves as an antioxidant, all of which are important in cancer prevention and treatment.[64,65] Studies have made the connection between Q10 deficiency and increased risk of breast cancer and melanoma.[66]

---

64 Sakano, K., et al." Suppression of Azoxymethane-Induced Colonic Premalignant Lesion Formation by Coenzyme Q10 in Rats." *Asian Pacific Journal of Cancer Prevention*, October 2006.

65 Rusciani, L., et al." Recombinant Interferon Alpha-2b and Coenzyme Q10 as a Postsurgical Adjuvant Therapy for Melanoma: A 3-Year Trial with Recombinant Interferon-Alpha and 5-Year Follow-Up." *Melanoma Research*, June 2007.

66 Folklers, K., et al." Activities of Vitamin Q10 in Animal Models and a Serious Deficiency in Patients with Cancer." *Biochemical and Biophysical Research Communications*, May 1997.

Coffee Berry Extract: I've mentioned tea so I also have to mention coffee, which also has health enhancing properties. I'm referring to the entire fruit, not only the bean or seed. The fruit is chock full of advantageous antioxidants, which, as we know, forestall the creation of deadly free radicals.

Dandelion Extract: While type II diabetics have too much glucose in their blood because cells are resisting the insulin that would shepherd the excess glucose into them and out of the blood, dandelion, with its active compound inulin, works against this effect of diabetes by trapping glucose molecules, stopping them from reaching high concentrations in the blood. Reports indicate that dandelion extracts reduce blood sugar levels by as much as 20 percent in a short period of time.

DHEA: DHEA, a naturally occurring steroid that is produced by the adrenal glands, has some reported effects on reducing cholesterol and abating depression, although these effects are still under study. One valuable experiment was a six-month investigation of elderly people, who were given DHEA, with the end result that they significantly reduced abdominal fat and improved insulin action.

Dimethyl Sulfoxide (DMSO): By suppressing TNF-alpha and NF-kB, dimethyl sulfoxide (DMSO) blocks the production of damaging cytokines. The combination of shark cartilage, vitamin C, and DMSO has been reported to heal basal cell carcinoma.[67]

EPA/DHA: I now want to signal the special benefits of one particular fatty acid, DHA, which is helpful to diabetes sufferers who also are plagued by obesity. A study looked at overweight patients, who were started on DHEA, which they took daily for three months. Then this dosage was supplemented with DHA (docosahexaenoic acid), one of the fatty acids found in fish oil, and in many cases there was a significant improvement in the level of insulin sensitivity.

---

67 Null, Gary. *The Complete Encyclopedia of Natural Healing*. New York: Kensington, 1998.

Essential Fatty Acids (EFAs): EFAs are the precursors to hormones in the body and, as such, are crucial for both men and women. It is especially necessary for those who have a low-fat diet to ensure that they are receiving adequate amounts of EFAs. Sesame, pumpkin, and safflower oils are all good sources of omega-6s. Walnut, flax, and chia are high in omega-3s. Ideally, your diet should balance omega 3s with omega 6s in a 1:1 ratio. Omega-3 fatty acids block important causes of cancer. Omega-3 fatty acids can suppress dangerous cytokines, as well as the stress-induced pro-inflammatory cytokines IL-6 and IL-10. While some fish oils are a rich source of Omega-3s and have been found to reduce the risk of skin, breast, and prostate cancer,[68,69,70] not all fish have a good Omega-3/Omega 6 ratio, and it is important to know where fish came from and to avoid farmed fish at all costs. Remember, fish don't synthesize Omega-3 fatty acids on their own; they obtain it from eating green vegetable matter. So boosting your intake of green leafy vegetables with high Omega-3 contents will also provide high dietary levels of this valuable antioxidant.

Evening Primrose Oil: Our brief examination of alpha lipoic acid noted that it counteracted the nerve damage associated with the progression of diabetes. Such nerve disturbance can hurt the feet, hands, and other body parts. Evening primrose oil is also an effective agent in the battle to alleviate nerve injury. An eye-opening study done to look at this particular problem looked at over 100 patients with mild nerve damage from diabetes. They were given six capsules of gamma-linolenic acid—this is the effective agent found in the evening primrose—twice daily for a year. The control

---

68 Brown, M. D. "Promotion of Prostatic Metastatic Migration towards Human Bone Marrow Stoma by Omega 6 and Its Inhibition by Omega 3 PUFAs." *British Journal of Cancer* 94, no. 6 (2006): 842-53.

69 Gago-Dominguez, M. "Opposing Effects of Dietary n-3 and n-6 Fatty Acids on Mammary Carcinogenesis: The Singapore Chinese Health Study." *British Journal of Cancer* 89, no. 9 (2003): 1686-92.

70 MacLean, C., et al. "Effects of Omega-3 Fatty Acids on Cancer." *AHRQ Evidence Reports*, February 2005.

group was given a placebo. Sixteen measures of nerve function were charted. The group on gamma-linolenic acid improved in every category. In thirteen of the sixteen measures, the improvement was significant. This is convincing evidence of the value of this supplement.

Fiber Complex: Another substance that is well known in one of its properties is fiber. Older people are well aware that fiber promotes good digestion. However, like the just-mentioned proteolytic enzymes, fiber also has a less-known side. Taking sufficient amounts of fiber prevents and decreases the dangers caused by constantly elevated blood glucose. Its value in this respect was indicated by a study in which diabetics consumed 25 grams of soluble fiber and 25 grams of insoluble fiber daily. This high-fiber diet decreased blood glucose levels by an average of 10 percent. Now, you've got another reason to put this in your diet.

Flavonoids: Bright colors in fresh fruits and vegetables are usually indicative of flavonoids, which are phytochemicals that are efficient free radical scavengers. Citrin, hesperidin, quercetin, and rutin are names of some of these disease-fighting substances. Studies suggest that flavonoids help prevent damage to DNA, neutralize carcinogens, and lower the risk of lung cancer.[71,72,73]

Garlic: Throughout this book, we've seen that interconnectedness of diabetes with many other diseases. Garlic or, more precisely, its active ingredient allium, helps with a whole slew of these related health problems. Studies indicate it reduces the chance of cardiovascular disease as well as lowering

---

71 Knekt, Paul." Dietary Flavonoids and the Risk of Lung Cancer and Other Malignant Neoplasms." *American Journal of Epidemiology,* April 7, 1997.

72 Le Marchand, Loïc, et al. "Intake of Flavonoids and Lung Cancer." *Journal of the National Cancer Institute*, Nov. 15, 1999.

73 Cui, Y., et al. "Dietary Flavonoid Intake and Lung Cancer—A Population-Based Case-Control Study." *Cancer,* May 2008.

oxidative stress and blood pressure. Animal studies have noted that allium promotes weight loss and insulin sensitivity.

Ginkgo Biloba: Studies of ginkgo biloba have progressed beyond experiments on rodents up to human subjects and produced encouraging results in both cases. In animal studies, it was learned that ginkgo improved glucose metabolism in muscle fibers. Other tests on animals indicated that the ginkgo biloba brought down post-meal sugar levels. Not only did it, thus, strike at the root of the diabetes problem, which resides in excess glucose in the blood, but ginkgo has been found to fight the symptoms in that it prevented diabetic retinopathy (an eye disease) in rats with diabetes. Turning to human studies, let me note one in which type II diabetics were given 120 mg of ginkgo for three months. The subjects experienced enhanced liver functioning in relation to usage of insulin and oral hypoglycemic drugs, which was connected to a reduction in blood glucose levels.

Ginseng: A recent study by researchers from the University of Chicago that was published in *Diabetes,* argues that an extract from the ginseng root could be an effective part of an overall treatment regimen for diabetes and obesity. They found that a ginseng extract normalized blood glucose levels, improved insulin sensitivity, and lowered weight.

GLA: Since it has been established that diabetes and cardiovascular disease are closely linked, it is an especially encouraging note to see that GLA aids in combating both. The positive impact of GLA (and DHA) on the cardiovascular system have been well-documented, seen in modest, though steady declines in blood pressure and considerable decreases in serum lipids. It also has a beneficial role in decreasing cellular insulin resistance. While the first benefit mentioned, reducing blood pressure, relates to lowering the risk of heart disease, the last is more directly helpful to diabetics in that, as we've learned, insulin resistance is a major factor in the growth of diabetes.

Glutamine: Studies suggest that glutamine—the most abundant amino acid in the human body—may decrease tumor progression.[74] It also may stabilize weight loss by allowing better nutrient absorption.

Glutathione Peroxidase: Glutathione is found in every cell of our bodies, where it plays a major role in defending our systems. Studies show that low levels of glutathione increase the risk of cancer, AIDS, and chronic fatigue syndrome.[75] To stimulate glutathione production, L-glutathione and N-acetyl-cysteine (NAC, a precursor of glutathione) should be taken.

Grape Seed Extract: Grape seeds contain pycnogenol, a powerful disease-fighting antioxidant. Pycnogenol, among its various age-retardant abilities, slows cell mutations. Intake of grape seed extract has been linked with significant decreases in the risk of developing colon, prostate, and breast cancers.[76,77,78,79] In a landmark study, French researchers decided to see what would happen if they fed rodents a diet that contained 60 percent fructose. Not surprisingly, the rodents suffered a disastrous decline in health. Blood pressure shot through the roof, free radicals sped up, and the heart enlarged. However, the study was not conceived as a way to torment the animals, but to see what supplements could counteract these rapidly

---

74 Wise, D., and C. Thompson." Glutamine Addiction: A New Therapeutic Target in Cancer." *Trends in Biochemical Sciences,* 2010.

75 Null, Gary. *The Complete Encyclopedia of Natural Healing.* New York: Kensington, 1998.

76 Kaur, Manjinder, et al. "Anticancer and Cancer Chemopreventive Potential of Grape Seed Extract and Other Grape-Based Products." *Journal of Nutrition,* 2009.

77 Radhakrishnan, S. "Resveratrol Potentiates Grape Seed Extract Induced Human Colon Cancer Cell Apoptosis." *Frontiers in Bioscience,* June 2011.

78 Raina, Komal, et al. "Oral Grape Seed Extract Inhibits Prostate Tumor Growth and Progression in TRAMP Mice." *Cancer Research,* June 2007.

79 Chen, Changjie, et al. "Grape Seed Extract Inhibits Proliferation of Breast Cancer Cell MCF-7 and Decrease the Gene Expression of Survivin." *China Journal of Chinese Materia Medica,* April 2009.

declining health conditions. By study's end, all the negative effects of this diet were brought under control by a variety of the components of grapes. Anthocyanin, a part of the grape's skin, prevented heart enlargement and high blood pressure. Procyanidins, found in the seed portion, had a positive impact on triglycerides, and all the parts of the grape blocked free radicals. The application to the present subject is clear in that many of the rodents' symptoms of ill health, such as the presence of free radicals and high blood pressure, also accompany diabetes. This and other studies suggest the value of grape seed extracts in fighting the disease.

Green Tea Extract: Without covering what I have discussed in other works, let me just say briefly that nature is a storehouse of invaluable medicines, and many of the most famous, scientifically "discovered" wonder drugs are, in fact, plant derivatives. In green tea, the special derivative is epigallocatechins, which may well have a major part to play in preventing diabetes. While all its effectiveness may not be due to this compound, we also know that green tea extract suppresses diet-induced obesity and acts as a potent antioxidant, while blocking processes that would injure the pancreas and liver.

Gymnema Syvestre: Obviously, animal trials with drugs, vitamins and supplements are a first stage of determining the efficacy of the substance. Once any chemical has proven its value in treating animals, it will ideally be tested on humans. Gymnema has been tested particularly on mice, and its results with them have been most promising indeed. In rat trials, gymnema supported healthy blood sugar levels. These levels in normal and diabetic rats were lowered two hours after oral administration of a gymnema concentrate. Moreover, gymnema corrected hyperglycemia in mild diabetic rats, and considerably extended the lifespan of severe diabetic rats. Hopefully, studies with humans will confirm the importance of gymnema as an anti-diabetic agent.

Inositol: A number of scientific studies have shown that inositol, a naturally occurring substance found both in the human cells and in vegetable fiber, is a powerful anti-cancer agent. More recently, however, it has been shown to also be an asset in the fight against type II diabetes. A large number of studies are suggesting inositol is key in regulating healthy insulin production, and, as we know, when this production goes awry, diabetes is the likely outcome.

L-Carnitine: Supplementation with L-carnitine is especially valuable as it can improve insulin sensitivity in those with type II diabetes. Carnitine, along with CoQ10 and NADH, also fights against heart disease by enhancing energy uptake in the heart muscle.

L-Glutamine: Another study with mice looked simultaneously at diabetes and obesity. This study with rodents prone to obesity and diabetes reported that, after supplementing for one week with L-glutamine, the mice had a minimum 5 percent reduction in body weight and normalized insulin levels.

Magnesium Citrate: Diabetics frequently are deficient in magnesium, either as the result of medications or disease. One double-blind, placebo-controlled study revealed the downside of this deficiency. When the patients took magnesium supplements, this helped with their control of blood sugar, so its lack in diabetics is part of the reason for their imperfect blood sugar control.

Maitake Complex: Another medicinal food among the compounds on this list is maitake, a mushroom that has been used extensively in traditional Japanese and Chinese medicine. If the Asians got there first, in terms of learning of this plant's benefits, Western doctors now recognize it as a booster of the immune system. It has been useful in treating diabetes, high blood pressure, cholesterol, and obesity.

Manganese: In discussing the value of B6, I brought up its counteraction against glycation, a process that accelerates aging. Another key contributor to the deterioration normally associated with aging is the presence of free radicals, unbalanced cells, or molecules that disrupt biological functions. Increased free radical production has been found in diabetics. Manganese is a component of the antioxidant enzyme called manganese super oxide dismutase (Mn-SOD). All antioxidants destroy free radicals. A second benefit of manganese is found in its reduction of the threat of arteriosclerosis. LDL cholesterol poses a great danger to the blood vessels, gumming them up with plaque, and thus promoting constricted blood flow, which can lead to heart attack or stroke. However, cholesterol is a threat not in its natural but in its oxidized form. A study reported that diabetics with higher blood levels of manganese were better protected from the oxidation of LDL cholesterol than individuals with less manganese.

NAC: We must press forward into human studies with many of these compounds, but again with N-acetylcysteine, a powerful antioxidant, animal studies are the best we have. And they tell an encouraging story. In studies involving diabetic rats, NAC protected the heart from endothelial damage and oxidative stress, two conditions closely associated with heart attacks among diabetics. In another examination, NAC increased nitric oxide in diabetic rats, and this improved blood pressure and reduced oxidative stress levels in their hearts.

Potassium: We've seen that the keystone of diabetes is problems with availability of or the body's ability to use insulin. That is why potassium is so crucial. Studies show that potassium improves insulin secretion, sensitivity and responsiveness. And this counters the effects of insulin injection, which induces potassium loss. A high potassium intake also reduces the risk of heart disease, atherosclerosis, and cancer.

Proteolytic Enzymes: Enzymes are the body's catalysts, which promote specific chemical reactions, such as breaking down foods into usable components. The proteolytic enzymes, the major type, are ones that control reactions that govern proteins. Some natural health practitioners recommend taking them after meals to aid digestion. This is an efficient manner of getting enzymes into the diet. However, a lesser-known value of the proteolytic enzymes is that they reduce the inflammation connected with diabetes. That is why I am calling attention to them here.

Quercetin: I need to say one more thing about free radicals. Oxidation is a chemical reaction in the body that, like glycosylation, mentioned earlier, can be benign. However, it can also release free radicals. Antioxidants reduce oxidative reactions in the body and so forestall the creation of these radicals. Flavonoids, organic compounds derived from plants, are antioxidants that reduce the harm associated with diabetes. Quercetin, a powerful flavonoid, decreases levels of blood glucose and oxidants. Thus it battles against a chief feature of diabetes, excessive blood sugar, and of more general bodily distress, the presence of oxidants, which promote free radicals. In addition, quercetin normalizes the levels of the following antioxidants: vitamin C, superoxide dismutase and vitamin E.

R-Lipoic Acid: R-lipoic acid is another superhero among supplements, since it has a number of "superpowers." For one, it is a potent antioxidant. It enhance glucose uptake, the very thing that is wounded by diabetes, and resists glycoslylation, a process whose downside has already been noted. It also has anti-inflammation properties.

Sea Vegetable Powder: When you think of sea vegetables, probably the first one that comes to mind is kelp, which grows in giant "forests" under the sea. Kelp is a rich source of iodine, but so are the other sea vegetables. In the lead-up to this protocol list, I noted that some of the items on it strengthen the thyroid, which is an important benefit in that the thyroid regulates the body's overall metabolism. Any dysfunction in the thyroid will mess up the body's functioning big time. Sea vegetables play a role here in that they are rich sources of iodine, and this substance works to prevent thyroid diseases. Obviously, a body with a weakened thyroid will not be in an optimal place to combat diabetes and its related conditions, and so the iodine in sea vegetables is crucial here. Further, a diet that includes sea vegetables will benefit persons who have atherosclerosis or heart disease induced by diabetes.

Selenium: This trace element, which is involved in DNA metabolism and the health of all cell membranes, has antioxidant properties, promotes apoptosis (cancer cell destruction), acts as an immunological response modifier, and plays a part in cancer prevention and treatment.[80,81,82] Supplementation of selenium can improve the quality of life during aggressive cancer therapies. This vital mineral can be found in grains, garlic, and Brazil nuts. It is a powerful antioxidant that may protect against heart attack and stroke. Selenium appears to encourage a healthy cardiovascular system by increasing the ratio of good cholesterol (MDL) to bad cholesterol (LDL). A healthy cardiovascular system means a healthy flow of nutrient-rich blood to the brain.

Silibinin (Milk Thistle): The major active constituent of milk thistle is a long-recognized antioxidant that has recently discovered anticarcinogenic qualities.[83,84,85] Milk thistle is an adaptogenic herb. It produces repair where it's needed or shuts down cell production in tumor cells. Silibinin encourages differentiation in malignant cells, blocks the activity of the enzyme COX-2, and, by cutting off the vascular network of the tumor, inhibits the growth of drug-resistant breast and ovarian cancer lines.

---

80 Amaral, Andre, et al. "Selenium and Bladder Cancer Risk: A Meta-analysis." *Cancer Epidemiology, Biomarkers & Prevention*, August 2010.

81 Duffield-Lillico, A. J., et al. "Selenium Supplementation, Baseline Plasma Selenium Status and Incidence of Prostate Cancer: An Analysis of the Complete Treatment Period of the Nutritional Prevention of Cancer Trial." *BJU International* 91, no. 7 (2003): 608-12.

82 Bleys, J., et al. "Serum Selenium Levels and All-Cause, Cancer, and Cardiovascular Mortality among U.S. Adults." *Archives of Internal Medicine* 168, no. 4 (2008): 404-10.

83 Syed, Deeba, et al." Chemoprevention of Prostate Cancer through Dietary Agents: Progress and Promise." *Cancer Epidemiology, Biomarkers and Prevention*, November 2007.

84 Lah, J. J., W. Cui, and K. Q. Hu. "Effects and Mechanisms of Silibinin on Human Hepatomav Cell Lines." *World J Gastroenterol* 2007; 13(40): 5299-5305.

85 Kiefer, Dale. "Report: A New Weapon to Fight Prostate Cancer." *Life Extension Magazine*, November 2005. http://www.lef.org/magazine/mag2005/nov2005_report_prostate_01.htm (accessed March 3, 2012).

Silymarin: By this time, you may have seen through the method behind my protocol. Some of the recommended substances work all around, attacking diabetes and its accompanying illnesses, while others are poised to alleviate only one of the areas of stress. Silymarin is particularly pertinent in that it protects the liver. The extract from milk thistle, silymarin has as its most active compound silibinin. It enhances the liver's control of glucose as well as decreasing the free radicals that could bring about liver damage.

Superoxide Dismutase and Catalase: Much like glutathione, these antioxidants are frontline defenses against free radical damage, and are especially protective of the heart, brain, lungs, kidney, and liver.

Turmeric: Where aloe vera is found in many beauty care products, turmeric is common in food. It is an Asian spice mixed in many curries, and like many natural food additives that have a long history in regional histories, it also has medicinal properties, being known to reduce inflammation, heal wounds and ease pain. Inflammation has not been mentioned thus far but, to say a word about it, it has come to the attention of scientists recently that type II diabetes interferes with cytokines, agents of the immune system that cause inflammation. Moreover, it has been seen that these imbalances and the inflammation they spur are particularly prevalent in the obese. Animal studies have suggested that turmeric can both reduce the likelihood of the occurrence of adult-onset diabetes as well as the inflammation that is associated with it. Researchers from Columbia University found that mice treated with turmeric were less susceptible to developing Type II diabetes In addition, they came to learn that obese mice given turmeric reported considerably reduced inflammation in their liver and fat tissue as measured against the controls, who were not given the spice. These scientists hypothesized that the curcumin—the active, anti-inflammatory, antioxidant component in turmeric—interferes with the inflammatory response caused by obesity. With lowered inflammation, insulin resistance was also reduced and thus type II diabetes discouraged.

Vanadyl Sulfate: While I noted earlier that insulin injection, while necessary for those with type I diabetes, when used by those with type II can sometimes be counterproductive. I discussed that this use of added insulin can often be reduced or avoided, but I didn't mention an interesting fact, which is that the chemical vanadyl sulfate mimics insulin. Vanadium, the basic form of vanadyl sulfate, which works particularly with the muscles, and so is also of interest to bodybuilders, is believed to assist in the transfer of sugar in the blood (glucose) into muscles, just as insulin does. In addition, scientists believe it can increase insulin sensitivity in the muscles. These combined effects may show diabetics a natural way to lower blood sugar, decrease their insulin intake and, perhaps, stop using insulin.

Vitamin A: Vitamin A reduces infections and tumors, and is especially noteworthy for its ability to clear the lungs of smoke and other pollutants.[86,87,88] Studies of animals show a definitive link between vitamin A deficiency and higher cancer risk.[89,90] Emulsified vitamin A comes from fish oil and is easy to digest. Vitamin A also comes from non-animal sources, such as lemongrass, wheatgrass, and carrots. Because vitamin A is fat-soluble

---

86   Prakash, P., N. I. Krinsky, and R. M. Russell. "Retinoids, Carotenoids, and Human Breast Cancer Cell Cultures: A Review of Differential Effects." *Nutr Rev* 2000;58(6): 170-176.

87   "Vitamin A May Slash Melanoma Risk, Especially in Women." LiveScience. http://www.livescience.com/18755-melanoma-risk-vitamin-women.html (accessed March 28, 2012).

88   de Klerk, N. H., A. W. Musk, G. L. Ambrosini, et al. "Vitamin A and Cancer Prevention II: Comparison of the Effects of Retinol and Beta-carotene." *Int J Cancer*. 1998;75:362-367.

89   Sivakumaran, Muttuswamy. "Role of Vitamin A Deficiency in the Pathogenesis of Myeloproliferative Disorders." *Blood Journal*. http://bloodjournal.hematologylibrary.org/content/98/5/1636.full (accessed March 28, 2012).

90   Li, K., et al. "The Effect of Vitamin A Deficiency in Maternal Rats on Tumor Formation in Filial Rats." *Journal of Pediatric Surgery* 44, no. 3 (2009): 565-570. http://www.ncbi.nlm.nih.gov/pubmed/19302860 (accessed March 12, 2012).

and not excreted by the body, excessive intake can be dangerous, inducing hypervitaminosis A, which causes cells to swell and rupture, leading especially to central nervous system toxicity. But large quantities of vitamin A are needed for this to happen, and it is safe at the recommended dosage. Four thousand to 7,000 IU of vitamin A, from supplemental and food sources, are recommended daily—less if beta-carotene is taken.

Vitamin B Complex: The value of the vitamin B complex—a group of vitamins that includes thiamine, riboflavin, niacin, B-6, folate, B-12, pantothenic acid, biotin, and choline—in helping the body fight diseases has been so well documented in many books, that here I will simply underline its main features, which are that B complex vitamins reduce cholesterol and blood fat, both of great benefit to the diabetic; are important throughout all of life, but especially so during menopause; and play an important role in promoting brain health. Green vegetables and whole grains are good sources of B vitamins. Vitamins B5 and B6 are particularly good for menopausal women. One study reported that middle-age men who had the highest amounts of vitamin B6 in their blood scored best on memory tasks, as compared to other middle-age men who had B6 deficiencies.[16] Vitamin B6 is also thought to improve verbal memory and combat depression. Vitamin B9, better known as folic acid, or folate, is critical for brain health. Studies seem to indicate that up to 38 percent of adults who have been clinically diagnosed with depression are deficient in folic acid.[17] Additional research from the Universities of Oxford (England) and Bergen (Norway) report that low folate and low vitamin B12 levels are connected to an increased risk of developing Alzheimer's disease. Both studies concluded that the risk for eventually getting Alzheimer's can be dramatically reduced through supplementation of folate and vitamin B12.[18] I recommend that you take a vitamin B complex that provides the daily amounts of all B vitamins as listed on the chart that appears toward the end of this chapter.

Vitamin B6: A moment ago, in discussing vitamin C, its battle against glycation was mentioned without much explanation. For some reason, glycation is accelerated in the plasma of type II diabetics. Vitamin B6 is one of the most effective anti-glycating agents known. The main form of B6 is pyridoxine.

Vitamin B12: Another marker of disease that is present in diabetics is heightened homocysteine levels. Homocysteine is an amino acid whose presence in high levels in the body has been associated with cardiovascular disease. One example of this correlation was found in Japanese studies that reveal those with non-insulin-dependent diabetes, who have blood vessel problems, also have elevated homocysteine. When given 1,000 micrograms of vitamin B12 on a daily basis for three weeks, the patients in one study saw their homocysteine levels fall precipitously.

Vitamin C: A powerful antioxidant, vitamin C protects against inflammation within our bodies, working to protect our brains against the effects of poor blood flow associated with atherosclerosis. Because vitamin C is water soluble and rapidly excreted from the body, it is important that levels be replenished daily. Vitamin C is the prime nutrient when it comes to overall support of the immune system. When fighting cancer, large quantities are required both orally and intravenously. For decades studies have established the importance of vitamin C intake in preventing and reversing breast, gastric, ovarian, and many other forms of cancer.[91,92,93,94,95] High doses of intravenous vitamins C and A are associated with long-term

---

91   Roberts L. J., M. G. Traber, and B. Frei. "Vitamins E and C in the Prevention of Cardiovascular Disease and Cancer in Men." *Free Radic Biol Med* 2009;46(11):1558.

92   Zhang S., D. J. Hunter, M. R. Forman, et al. "Dietary Carotenoids and Vitamins A, C, and E and Risk of Breast Cancer." *J Natl Cancer Inst* 1999;91(6):547-556.

93   Feiz, H. R., and S. Mobarhan." Does Vitamin C Intake Slow the Progression of Gastric Cancer in Helicobacter pylori-Infected Populations?"*Nutr Rev* 2002;60(1):34-36.

94   Chen Q., M. G. Espey, A. Y. Sun, et al. "Pharmacologic Doses of AscorbateAct as a Prooxidant and Decrease Growth of Aggressive Tumor Xenografts in Mice." *Proc Natl Acad Sci* 2008;105(32):11105-11109.

95   Drisko, J. A., J. Chapman, and V. J. Hunter. "The Use of Antioxidants with First-Line Chemotherapy in Two Cases of Ovarian Cancer." *J Am Coll Nutr* 2003;22(2):118-123.

survival of a variety of cancers, even after they have metastasized. Despite claims that vitamin C may disrupt chemotherapy treatments, recent studies have established that vitamin C kills tumor cells without interfering with the effectiveness of chemotherapy.[96],[97] Vitamin C also has great value in counteracting diabetes-caused eye problems. The aqueous humor of the eye supplies its adjacent areas with vitamin C. As we've learned, in diabetes insulin is not functioning properly to move glucose out of the blood. The excess glucose in circulation may inhibit vitamin C uptake, and so the aqueous humor's protective role, which depends on vitamin C distribution, may be thwarted. Supplementing with vitamin C will supply this missing element and improve eye health. It should also be noted that taking vitamin C in mega-doses may lessen the negative effects of glycation (which I will discuss more thoroughly below in the section on vitamin B6). Vitamin C also alleviates other negative conditions through its enhancement of bodily activities. By improving blood flow and decreasing inflammation, for example, it is a blessing to diabetics with coronary artery disease. It also lowers blood pressure and improves blood vessel elasticity.

Vitamin D: Sunlight is the best way to get vitamin D. Supplemental forms of vitamin D are also available. However, these should be taken with caution, as there is such a thing as too much vitamin D. This vitamin is especially important for those living in or near highly polluted areas.

Vitamin E: Vitamin E (tocopherol) is an antioxidant that helps protect tissue from unhealthy oxidative free radicals, which can cause damage and lead to premature aging and the development of chronic diseases, such as cancer, Alzheimer's, and cataract formation. There are a number of forms of vitamin E. The most common vitamin E supplement is alpha

---

96 Gonzalez, Michael, et al. "Orthomolecular Oncology Review: Ascorbic Acid and Cancer 25 Years Later." *Integrated Cancer Therapies,* March 2005 4: 32-44.

97 Moss, Ralph. "Should Patients Undergoing Chemotherapy and Radiotherapy Be Prescribed Antioxidants?." *Integrative Cancer Therapies.* http://ict.sagepub.com/content/5/1/63.abstract (accessed March 28, 2012).

tocopherol. Recent studies, however, suggest that gamma-tocopherol is the most effective form of vitamin E. When choosing a vitamin E supplement, look for one containing compounds called tocotrienols, which synergistically combine with vitamin E to help protect our bodies against damaging processes. Tocotrienols also lower the levels of LDL (the dangerous form of cholesterol), which is an important risk factor for heart attack and stroke (remember, this directly affects the brain). I suggest that you choose a vitamin E supplement that has 400 IU of alpha-tocopherol, 200 mg of gamma tocopherol, and 65 mg of tocotrienols. Much like vitamin C, vitamin E prevents cancer by preventing free radical damage, and activating immune system cells against tumors and infections.[98,99] In clinical studies, 400 to 1,200 IU daily have been shown to help patients with breast or cervical cancer.[100] Vitamin E works especially well when taken in conjunction with 200 mcg of selenium. Vitamin E has multiple benefits for perimenopausal women. For those still menstruating, vitamin E rejuvenates the immune system. It also helps alleviate hot flashes, lessen vaginal thinning, and reduce dryness. The best vitamin E is a mix of beta-, delta-, and gamma-tocopherols, as these are found together in nature. These are better sources than synthetic vitamin E. Furthermore, Vitamin E not only improves the health of diabetes sufferers but its lack in the body has been linked to the disease's occurrence. This vitamin also registers a positive impact on persons who already have diabetes. A study in *Diabetes Care* demonstrated that just one month of vitamin E administration reduced protein glycosylation. Glycosylation, which is an enzymatic process of linking proteins and other compounds, can be benign, but can also interfere with normal cellular processes. The most common form of vitamin E is alpha tocopherol. However, we have

---

98 "Vitamin E." Linus Pauling Institute at Oregon State University. http://lpi.oregon-state.edu/infocenter/vitamins/vitaminE/ (accessed March 21, 2012).

99 "Vitamin E in Front Line of Prostate Cancer Fight." Science Daily. http://www.sciencedaily.com/releases/2010/10/101019111718.htm (accessed March 8, 2012).

100 Null, Gary. *The Complete Encyclopedia of Natural Healing*. New York: Kensington, 1998.

found that gamma, mixed tocopherols, and a full range of tocotrienols are more beneficial for diabetes.

Vitamin K: Mounting evidences points to vitamin K, a potent antioxidant with anti-inflammatory properties, as a powerful tool in the prevention and treatment of cancer. Abundant in leafy greens, vitamin K has been shown to inhibit the progression of liver cancers and shows great promise for treating numerous types of cancer, including prostate and lung cancer.[101,102,103]

Zinc: Zinc plays a central role in keeping the immune system strong and maintaining healthy bones. This mineral is also important for proper function of the ovaries. Zinc deficiency is common in the United States, especially among the elderly. Women are more susceptible than men to the dangers of diabetes. As far as studies have looked into this, they have shown that increased zinc intake is connected to a reduced risk of type II diabetes in women.

---

101 Li, L., et al.; "Induction of Apoptosis in Hepatocellular Carcinoma Smmc-7721 Cells by Vitamin K(2) is Associated with p53 and Independent of the Intrinsic Apoptotic Pathway." *Molecular and Cellular Biochemistry,* September 2010.

102 Nimptsch, Katharina. "Dietary Vitamin K Intake in Relation to Cancer Incidence and Mortality: Results from the Heidelberg Cohort of the European Prospective Investigation into Cancer and Nutrition." *American Journal of Clinical Nutrition* 10.3945 (2010). http://www.ajcn.org/content/early/2010/03/24/ajcn.2009.28691.abstract (accessed March 13, 2012).

103 Kaneda, M., D. Zhang, R. Bhattacharjee, K. Nakahama, S. Arii, and I. Morita." Vitamin K2 Suppresses Malignancy of HuH7 Hepatoma Cells via Inhibition of Connexin 43." *Cancer Lett* 2008;263:53-60.

Index

Fahrenheit	Celcius	Gas Mark
225°	110°	¼
250°	120°	½
275°	140°	1
300°	150°	2
325°	160°	3
350°	180°	4
375°	190°	5
400°	200°	6
425°	220°	7
450°	230°	8

METRIC AND IMPERIAL CONVERSIONS
(These conversions are rounded for convenience)

Ingredient	Cups/Tablespoons/ Teaspoons	Ounces	Grams/Milliliters
Coconut Oil	1 cup=16 tablespoons	7.5 ounces	209 grams
Cheese, non-dairy, shredded	1 cup	4 ounces	110 grams
Flour, all-purpose	1 cup/1 tablespoon	4.5 ounces/0.3 ounces	125 grams/8 grams
Fruit, dried	1 cup	4 ounces	120 grams
Fruits or veggies, chopped	1 cup	5 to 7 ounces	145 to 200 grams
Fruits or veggies, puréed	1 cup	8.5 ounces	245 grams
Honey or maple syrup	1 tablespoon	.75 ounces	20 grams
Liquids: nut milks, water, or juice	1 cup	8 fluid ounces	240 milliliters
Oats	1 cup	5.5 ounces	150 grams
Quinoa, uncooked	1 cup	6 ounces	170 grams
Salt	1 teaspoon	0.2 ounces	6 grams
Spices: cinnamon, cloves, ginger, or nutmeg (ground)	1 teaspoon	0.2 ounces	5 milliliters
Vanilla extract	1 teaspoon	0.2 ounces	4 grams